BLOOM
Founded by | arihant

Olympiad ACE

A Comprehensive Practice Book

for School Olympiads & Talent Search Exams

GENERAL KNOWLEDGE

Class 7

by
Suman Bharti

Olympiad ACE

BLOOM

Bloom Cap Edu Ventures Pvt. Ltd.

Administrative & Production Office

'Ramchhaya' 4577/15, Agarwal Road, Darya Ganj, New Delhi -110002
Tele: 011- 47630600, 43518550

PRICE: ₹125.00

PO No. : TXT-59-T067228-09-25

Published by Arihant Publications (I) Ltd.

For further information about the books log on to
www.bloomcap.org

Follow us on

Preface

"Future belongs to those Who prepares for it today"

School Olympiads are National & International level competitions conducted by different Government, Non-Government & Educational Organisations with the purpose of making the children ready to face competitive exams.
The challenging Questions asked in Olympiads motivate them to learn more & more and bring out the best result with improved academic performance.
The Awards & Scholarship offered by Olympiads motivate children to aspire & strive for doing better and emerge out to be the best.

GK Olympiads

GK is the knowledge of every aspect of the human life, which may or may not be the part of routine academic studies but very important for the overall personality development of the students. It is more or less connected with the attentiveness and awareness. There can be different domains of GK like; History, Geography, Polity, Culture, Discovery, Sports, Current Affairs etc.
GK Olympiads help students in understanding the importance of General Knowledge and updations about National & International Affairs in daily life.

'Bloom GK Olympiad Study Book Class 7' is a perfect resource to Study & Practice for Olympiad Exams and other National & State Level Talent Search Exams & Other Competitions.

Some Special Features of Bloom GK Olympiad Study Books are;

- Complete coverage of all the topics related to GK;. History, Geography, Environment, Polity, Science, Sports, etc.
- Chapterwise Exercises having different types of Objective Questions.
- Olympiad Pattern Practice Sets at the end.

This book is prepared by Expert Panel with the utmost care, still if you have any suggestions regarding its improvement then feel free to contact us at support@bloomcap.org. We will try to inculcate your suggestions in the further editions.

Contents

Chapter

01

History of India and the World

MCQs 1 Mark Questions

1. Who among the following is known as the 'Napoleon of India'?
(a) Samudragupta (b) Ashoka
(c) Chandragupta (d) Kumaragupta

2. Identify the famous ruler/king who is also known as the 'Second Ashoka'.
(a) Vasudeva (b) Kanishka
(c) Shishunaga (d) Vikramaditya

3. Complete the given analogy.
Sun Temple : Konark : : Lingaraj Temple : ?
(a) Sambalpur (b) Puri
(c) Bhubaneswar (d) Cuttack

4. Charak was the famous court physician of which among the following kings?
(a) Harshavardhana
(b) Chandragupta Maurya
(c) Ashoka
(d) Kanishka

5. The Chinese traveller Fa-Hein came to India during the reign of which of the following Gupta Kings?
(a) Skandagupta (b) Chandragupta II
(c) Samudragupta (d) Kumaragupta I

6. Who was the founder of the Rashtrakutas dynasty?
(a) Dantidurga (b) Harshavardhana
(c) Prithviraja III (d) Amoghavarsha I

7. Identify the incorrectly matched pair.

	Dynasty		Region
(a)	Gurjara-Pratiharas	–	Northern and Western India
(b)	Rashtrakutas	–	Bengal
(c)	Palas	–	Bihar and Bengal
(d)	Cholas	–	Tamil Nadu

8. ………… was an ambassador who was sent to the court of Chandragupta Maurya by the Greek ruler 'Seleucus Nicator'.
(a) Megasthenes (b) Fattien
(c) Hiuen Tsang (d) Strabo

9. Which of the following dynasties were involved in the tripartite struggle for control of Northern India in the 9th century?
(a) Palas, Pratiharas and Chalukyas
(b) Sena, Rashtrakutas and Pratiharas
(c) Palas, Pratiharas and Rashtrakutas
(d) Palas, Sena and Chalukyas

10. The temple of Thanjavur and Gangaikondacholapuram were built by .... and ....
(a) Ashoka, Kanishka
(b) Vasudeva, Ashoka
(c) Vijayalaya, Kulottunga
(d) Rajaraja, Rajendra

11. Identify the ruler who built the Konark Sun Temple.
(a) Narasimhadeva I (b) Krishna I
(c) Mihir Bhoja (d) Veera Ballala

12. Who was the first slave king of Delhi Sultanate?
(a) Iltutmish
(b) Qutb-ud-Din Aibak
(c) Ghiyas-ud-din Balban
(d) Alauddin Khalji

13. Which of the following was not a Rajput dynasty?
(a) Solankis (b) Chauhans
(c) Rashtrakutas (d) Chandelas

14. Consider the following regarding the advent of Europeans in India and choose the correct chronological order.
(a) Portuguese, English, Dutch
(b) English, Portuguese, Dutch
(c) Portuguese, Dutch, English
(d) English, Dutch, Portuguese

15. When Babur attacked India, the Sultanate was under the rule of ....
(a) Akbar (b) Sher Shah
(c) Ibrahim Lodi (d) Maharana Pratap

16. Name the Mughal ruler who was exiled to Burma.
(a) Bahadur Shah Zafar (b) Shah Jahan
(c) Babur (d) Akbar

17. Identify the Mughal Emperor who became ruler at the age of thirteen years.
(a) Babur (b) Shah Jahan
(c) Akbar (d) Jahangir

18. Which among the following Maratha kings had a council of minister of 8 members known as Astha Pradhan?
(a) Shivaji (b) King Shahu
(c) Sambhaji (d) Tarabai

19. The second Battle of Panipat was fought between which among the following rulers?
(a) Akbar and Hemu
(b) Akbar and Maharana Pratap
(c) Humayun and Sher Shah
(d) Babur and Ibrahim Lodi

20. Who was the author of 'Humayun-Nama'?
(a) Abu'l Fazl (b) Birbal
(c) Gulbadan Begum (d) Tansen

21. Which of the following kings built the Purana Qila in Delhi?
(a) Humayun (b) Babur
(c) Akbar (d) Sher Shah Suri

22. Identify the following personality who gave the famous slogan 'Do or Die'.
(a) Jawaharlal Nehru (b) Sardar Patel
(c) Mahatma Gandhi (d) Bhagat Singh

23. The British East India Company captured Puducherry from the French in which of the following years?
(a) 1761 (b) 1699 (c) 1767 (d) 1628

24. Identify the incorrectly matched pair.
(a) Francis Day – Denmark
(b) Colbert – Denmark
(c) Captain Hawkins – Britain
(d) Pedro Cabral – Portugal

25. Identify the person shown in the picture given below, who was the first European to reach India by sea route via the Cape of Good Hope on 20th May, 1498 at Kappad near Calicut on the Malabar Coast of India.

(a) Marco Polo (b) Megasthenes
(c) Al-Masudi (d) Vasco da Gama

26. Which among the following civilisations is the oldest in the world?
(a) Mesopotamian Civilisation
(b) Egyptian Civilisation
(c) Indus Valley Civilisation
(d) Chinese Civilisation

27. Alexander the Great, became the king of Macedonia in which year?
(a) 323 BC (b) 336 BC
(c) 350 BC (d) 200 BC

28. What was the name of the Indian King who fought with Alexander the Great?
(a) Chandragupta Maurya (b) Ashoka
(c) King Porus (d) Bimbisara

29. Christopher Colombus discover America in which year?
(a) 1490 (b) 1489 (c) 1491 (d) 1492

30. Which of the following countries signed the Peace of Treaty (1917) with Germany during the First World War?
(a) Russia (b) Austria
(c) USA (d) England

31. When did United Kingdom declare war on Germany which led to Second World War?
(a) 4th April, 1939 (b) 3rd September, 1939
(c) 18th April, 1939 (d) 28th August, 1939

32. Which among the following treaties acknowledge the independence of America?
(a) Treaty of Versailles
(b) Treaty of France
(c) Treaty of Paris
(d) Treaty of America

33. What was the immediate cause of the beginning of the First World War?
(a) The Murder of William I
(b) The Murder of Victor Emmanuel II
(c) The Murder of William II
(d) The Murder of Archduke Ferdinand

MCQs 2 Marks Questions

34. Consider the following statements and select the correct option.
I. The Shatapatha Brahmana and Taittiriya Brahmana are the Brahmana texts of Yajurveda.
II. The Rigveda is the oldest text in the world.

Codes
(a) Only I (b) Only II
(c) Both I and II (d) Neither I nor II

35. Read the following statements and identifies which ones are true (T) and which ones are false (F).
I. Abu'l Fazl wrote Akbarnama.
II. Akbar patronised Tansen of Gwalior who composed many ragas.
III. Akbar constructed Humayun's tomb in Delhi.

Codes

	I	II	III		I	II	III
(a)	T	T	F	(b)	T	F	T
(c)	F	F	T	(d)	F	T	F

36. Identify the famous personality with the help of the information given below.
- I am the greatest ruler of the Vijayanagara Empire.
- I am popularly known as 'Andhra Bhoja'.

(a) Vira Narasimha Raya
(b) Krishnadeva Raya
(c) Achyota Deva Raya
(d) Sada Sina Raja

37. Match the following.

	List I		List II
A.	First World War	1.	1939-1945
B.	Second World War	2.	1789-1799
C.	The Great Depression	3.	1914-1918
D.	French Revolution	4.	1929-1930

Codes

	A	B	C	D
(a)	3	1	4	2
(b)	3	4	1	2
(c)	4	1	3	2
(d)	4	3	1	2

38. Consider the following statements and select the correct option.

I. The Printing Press in India was set up by Portuguese at Goa in 1550.

II. Portuguese were the last to leave from India.

Codes

(a) Only I
(b) Only II
(c) Both I and II
(d) Neither I nor II

39. Read the following statements and identifies which ones are true (T) and which ones are false (F).

I. Coins are good source to know about Administrative History.

II. The National Archives of India is located in New Delhi.

III. The Dutch founded their first factory at Masulipatnam in 1605.

Codes

	I	II	III		I	II	III
(a)	T	F	T	(b)	F	T	F
(c)	F	F	T	(d)	T	T	T

40. There are two statements marked as Assertion (A) and Reason (R). Mark your answer as per the codes given below.

Assertion (A) Ibrahim Lodi was the king of the Lodi dynasty and the last Sultan of Delhi.

Reason (R) He was defeated and killed at the Battle of Panipat by Babur's invading army, giving way to the emergence of the Mughal Empire in India.

Codes

(a) Both A and R are true and R is the correct explanation of A
(b) Both A and R are true, but R is not the correct explanation of A
(c) A is true, but R is false
(d) A is false, but R is true

41. Consider the following statements and select the correct option.

I. Iltutmish is regarded as the 'real founder of the Delhi Sultanate.

II. Iltutmish set up an official nobility of slaves known as Chalisa (group of 40).

III. Iltutmish completed the construction of Qutub Minar which was started by Aibak.

Codes

(a) I and II (b) II and III
(c) Only I (d) I, II and III

Darken your choice with HB Pencil

1.	a	b	c	d	8.	a	b	c	d	15.	a	b	c	d	22.	a	b	c	d	29.	a	b	c	d	36.	a	b	c	d
2.	a	b	c	d	9.	a	b	c	d	16.	a	b	c	d	23.	a	b	c	d	30.	a	b	c	d	37.	a	b	c	d
3.	a	b	c	d	10.	a	b	c	d	17.	a	b	c	d	24.	a	b	c	d	31.	a	b	c	d	38.	a	b	c	d
4.	a	b	c	d	11.	a	b	c	d	18.	a	b	c	d	25.	a	b	c	d	32.	a	b	c	d	39.	a	b	c	d
5.	a	b	c	d	12.	a	b	c	d	19.	a	b	c	d	26.	a	b	c	d	33.	a	b	c	d	40.	a	b	c	d
6.	a	b	c	d	13.	a	b	c	d	20.	a	b	c	d	27.	a	b	c	d	34.	a	b	c	d	41.	a	b	c	d
7.	a	b	c	d	14.	a	b	c	d	21.	a	b	c	d	28.	a	b	c	d	35.	a	b	c	d					

Chapter 02

Tribal Communities in India

MCQs 1 Mark Questions

1. In which state, Garo Khasi and Jaintia tribes are located?
   (a) Assam
   (b) Meghalaya
   (c) Madhya Pradesh
   (d) None of the above

2. In which among the following states the maximum number of tribes resides in India?
   (a) Bihar (b) Odisha
   (c) Madhya Pradesh (d) Jharkhand

3. Mundas are tribal group of .... region.
   (a) Andhra Pradesh
   (b) Telangana
   (c) Arunachal Pradesh
   (d) Jharkhand

4. Complete the given analogy.
   Lepcha : Sikkim : : Jaunsari : ?
   (a) Rajasthan (b) Uttarakhand
   (c) Tripura (d) Telangana

5. Identify the name of the largest tribe of India, as per the census 2011.
   (a) Bhil (b) Moplahs
   (c) Gond (d) Santhals

6. Which state has the largest population of Santhals?
   (a) Jharkhand (b) Arunachal Pradesh
   (c) Rajasthan (d) None of these

7. The Ahom tribes resides in which of the following states of India?
   (a) Sikkim (b) Nagaland
   (c) Assam (d) Madhya Pradesh

8. Where is the largest residence area of Lepcha and Bhutia tribes located?
   (a) Sikkim (b) Andhra Pradesh
   (c) Gujarat (d) Maharashtra

9. Bhagoriya is a tribal folk dance of native 'Baiga tribe' in which of the following states?
   (a) Gujarat (b) Himachal Pradesh
   (c) Tamil Nadu (d) Madhya Pradesh

10. Which tribe celebrated the Sarhul festival?
    (a) Oraon (b) Baiga
    (c) Gond (d) Bhils

11. 'Kalbelia' is a dance form, performed by the Kalbelia tribe in which state of India?
    (a) Rajasthan (b) Madhya Pradesh
    (c) Uttar Pradesh (d) Uttarakhand

12. Gaddi and Bakarwal are the famous tribes of which among the following states of India?
(a) Jammu and Kashmir
(b) Madhya Pradesh
(c) Jharkhand
(d) Uttar Pradesh

13. Mongols were hunter-gatherers tribes inhabited in ....
(a) Western Asia (b) South-East Asia
(c) South Asia (d) Central Asia

14. Tribe is one of India's largest scheduled tribes, which lives mainly in the state of Jharkhand.
(a) Bhil (b) Oraon
(c) Munda (d) Kuki

15. By which names, the santhals used to call the outsiders.
(a) Damin (b) Dikus
(c) Kayali (d) Chenchus

16. Which revolt was made famous by Bankim Chandra Chatterjee in his novel Anandamath?
(a) Munda Rebellion (b) Bhil Rebellion
(c) Sannyasi Rebellion (d) Ramosi Rebellion

17. Which of the following is the correct chronology order?
(a) Santhal Rebellion – Munda Rebellion – Tana Bhagat Rebellion
(b) Tana Bhagat Rebellion – Santhal Rebellion – Munda Rebellion
(c) Munda Rebellion – Tana Bhagat Rebellion – Santhal Rebellion
(d) Santhal rebellion – Tana Bhagat Rebellion – Munda Rebellion

18. Which one of the following tribes of India belongs to the proto-Australoid race?
(a) Santhal (b) Bhil
(c) Both (a) and (b) (d) Gond

19. Khokhar tribes lived in which among the following states of India?
(a) Assam
(b) Tamil Nadu
(c) Punjab
(d) Jammu and Kashmir

20. The Moplah tribe are mainly found in which of the following states of India?
(a) Kerala (b) Chhattisgarh
(c) Odisha (d) Jharkhand

MCQs 2 Marks Questions

21. Read the given statements and identifies which ones are true (T) and which ones are false (F).
I. Maize is the staple crop of Bhil tribe of Rajasthan.
II. The word 'Munda' means headman of a village.
III. Gair dance originated from Gond community of Rajasthan.
IV. Agriculture is the main occupation of the Gond tribes.

Codes

	I	II	III	IV
(a)	T	T	F	T
(b)	F	T	T	F
(c)	T	T	T	T
(d)	F	F	T	T

22. Consider the following statements and select the correct option.
I. Santhal revolt took place under the leadership of two brothers, Sindhu and Kanhu in 1855.
II. Rampa revolt was a tribal uprising led by Alluri Sitarama Raju in 1922.

Codes
(a) Only I
(b) Only II
(c) Both I and II
(d) Neither I nor II

23. Consider the following statements related to the Kol uprising and choose the correct option.

I. The Kol uprising was a tribal revolt of the Kol people of Chota Nagpur region in Jharkhand, during 1829-1939 against British policies.

II. The Kol uprising were under the leadership of Buddhu Bhagat.

Codes

(a) Only I (b) Only II

(c) Both I and II (d) Neither I nor II

24. There are two statements marked as Assertion (A) and Reason (R). Mark your answer as per the codes given below.

Assertion (A) Munda tribe are the largest and one of the oldest tribes in India,

Reason (R) The Munda are a tribe belonging to the Chota Nagpur plateau, spread across, Jharkhand, Chhattisgarh, Madhya Pradesh, Odisha, Tripura and West Bengal.

Codes

(a) Both A and R are true and R is the correct explanation of A

(b) Both A and R are true, but R is not the correct explanation of A

(c) A is true, but R is false

(d) A is false, but R is true

25. Match the following.

List I	List II
A. Gond	1. Assam
B. Bodo	2. Mizoram
C. Kuki	3. Madhya Pradesh
D. Khasi	4. Meghalaya

Codes

	A	B	C	D
(a)	3	1	2	4
(b)	2	1	4	3
(c)	3	1	4	2
(d)	4	2	3	1

Darken your choice with HB Pencil

1.	ⓐ ⓑ ⓒ ⓓ	6.	ⓐ ⓑ ⓒ ⓓ	11.	ⓐ ⓑ ⓒ ⓓ	16.	ⓐ ⓑ ⓒ ⓓ	21.	ⓐ ⓑ ⓒ ⓓ
2.	ⓐ ⓑ ⓒ ⓓ	7.	ⓐ ⓑ ⓒ ⓓ	12.	ⓐ ⓑ ⓒ ⓓ	17.	ⓐ ⓑ ⓒ ⓓ	22.	ⓐ ⓑ ⓒ ⓓ
3.	ⓐ ⓑ ⓒ ⓓ	8.	ⓐ ⓑ ⓒ ⓓ	13.	ⓐ ⓑ ⓒ ⓓ	18.	ⓐ ⓑ ⓒ ⓓ	23.	ⓐ ⓑ ⓒ ⓓ
4.	ⓐ ⓑ ⓒ ⓓ	9.	ⓐ ⓑ ⓒ ⓓ	14.	ⓐ ⓑ ⓒ ⓓ	19.	ⓐ ⓑ ⓒ ⓓ	24.	ⓐ ⓑ ⓒ ⓓ
5.	ⓐ ⓑ ⓒ ⓓ	10.	ⓐ ⓑ ⓒ ⓓ	15.	ⓐ ⓑ ⓒ ⓓ	20.	ⓐ ⓑ ⓒ ⓓ	25.	ⓐ ⓑ ⓒ ⓓ

Chapter

03

Art and Culture

MCQs 1 Mark Questions

1. Which of the following monuments was constructed to welcome King George and Queen Mary to India?
(a) Gateway of India
(b) Buland Darwaza
(c) Victoria Memorial
(d) India Gate

2. Identify the name of the famous personality who compose the Allahabad Pillar Inscription.
(a) Dandin (b) Harisena
(c) Sudraka (d) Banabhatta

The painting on the walls and ceilings in the Ajanta Caves depict mainly the incidents related to ....
(a) the Ramayana and Mahabharata
(b) the life of Mahavira
(c) the life of Gautam Buddha
(d) None of the above

4. The Rath Temple at Mahabalipuram was built by which of the following dynasties?
(a) Cholas (b) Chalukyas
(c) Pallavas (d) Rashtrakutas

5. The entrance gateways found at the temple of South India are called ....
(a) Mandaps (b) Devalayas
(c) Shikhars (d) Gopurams

6. Identify the temple as depicted in the picture given below.

(a) Brihadeshwara Temple
(b) Lingaraj Temple
(c) Akshardham Temple
(d) Badrinath Temple

7. Name the ruler who built the Vittala Temple of Hampi.
(a) Devaraya II (b) Krishnadeva Raya
(c) Vijaya Raya II (d) Harihara

8. The statue of Gomateshwara (Bahubali) is located in which state?
(a) Odisha (b) Karnataka
(c) Tamil Nadu (d) None of these

9. Tawang monastery, the largest monastery in India is located in ....
(a) Ladakh (b) Sikkim
(c) Arunachal Pradesh (d) Manipur

10. Which among the following is the largest and tallest surviving temple in Odisha?
(a) Rajarani Temple
(b) Bramheswara Temple
(c) Lingaraj Temple
(d) Jagannath Temple

11. Which lord is the main deity of Kandariya Mahadeva temple?
(a) Lord Shiva (b) Lord Vishnu
(c) Lord Brahma (d) Lord Ram

12. Which one of the following types of painting originated in the Indian state of Andhra Pradesh?
(a) Kalamkari Painting
(b) Madhubani Painting
(c) Kalighat Painting
(d) None of the above

13. Which of the following temples was/were constructed at Khajuraho?
(a) Jain Temple (b) Vaishnavite Temple
(c) Saivite Temple (d) All of these

14. In which of the following festivals are boat races a special feature?
(a) Pongal (b) Navratri
(c) Rongali Bihu (d) Onam

15. 'Khajuraho Dance Festival' is a famous event organised in which Indian state?
(a) Gujarat (b) Bihar
(c) Madhya Pradesh
(d) Maharashtra

16. .... is the harvest festival that is celebrated in Assam which marks the beginning of the Assamese New Year.
(a) Bihu (b) Lohri
(c) Makar Sankranti (d) Onam

17. Rouf folk dance belongs to which of the following states?
(a) Jammu and Kashmir
(b) Ladakh
(c) Himachal Pradesh
(d) Punjab

18. Identify the name of the personality who invented sitar.
(a) Tansen (b) Ali Akbar Khan
(c) Amir Khusrau (d) Bahadur Shah Zafar

19. Gurmukhi, Dogri and Sindhi scripts have developed from which among the following scripts?
(a) Brahmi Script (b) Sarada Script
(c) Kushana Script (d) Tankari Script

20. It is one of the eight classical dance form that originated in the Andhra Pradesh and largely developed as a Hindu God Krishna oriented vaishnanism tradition.
(a) Kuchipudi (b) Odissi
(c) Kathak (d) Sattriya

21. Identify the name of ancient sage who is considered as the Father of Natya Shastra.
(a) Bharata Muni (b) Bhaskaracharya
(c) Acharya Charak (d) Kapila

22. Identify the incorrectly matched pair.

	Classical Dance		State
(a)	Bharatanatyam	–	Tamil Nadu
(b)	Mohiniyattam	–	Kerala
(c)	Kathak	–	Uttar Pradesh
(d)	Kathakali	–	Odisha

MCQs 2 Marks Questions

23. Consider the following statements and select the correct option.
I. Nayanar Saints were devoted to Lord Shiva.
II. Tulsidas' composition Ramcharitmanas is written in Awadhi.
III. Alvar Saints were dedicated to Lord Vishnu.

Codes
(a) I and II (b) II and III
(c) I, II and III (d) None of these

24. Consider the following statements and select the correct option.
I. Mirabai become a disciple of Ravidas.
II. Ramanuja was a bhakti saint, who founded Vaishnav tradition.

Codes

(a) Only I (b) Only II
(c) Both I and II (d) Neither I nor II

25. Read the given statements and identifies which ones are true (T) and which ones are false (F).

I. The Shore Temple at Mahabalipuram was built by Chola Empire.
II. The temple of Thanjavur in Tamil Nadu was built by Raja Raja I.
III. Gol Gumbaz has the largest dome in India.
IV. The temple of Khajuraho was built by the Chandela Dynasty.

Codes

	I	II	III	IV		I	II	III	IV
(a)	F	F	F	T	(b)	T	T	T	T
(c)	F	F	F	F	(d)	F	T	F	T

26. Identify the name of the eminent personality with the help of the information given below.

- He was renowned Indian musician who played the Shehnai, musical instrument.
- He was awarded India's highest civilian honour award the Bharat Ratna in 2001.

(a) Bhimsen Joshi
(b) Bismillah Khan
(c) Hariprasad Chaurasia
(d) Amjad Ali Khan

27. Identify the famous personality with the help of the information given below.

I. He was renowned Indian poet and world's best Sanskrit poet from the Gupta period during 5th century AD.
II. He was considered as Shakespeare of the East. His work includes Raghuvamsa, Meghadutam, Ritusamhara and many other.

(a) Aryabhatta (b) Kalidas
(c) Vatsyayana (d) Varahamihira

28. There are two statements marked as Assertion (A) and Reason (R). Mark your answer as per the codes given below.

Assertion (A) Baisakhi is an important festival for the people of Sikh religion.

Reason (R) It commemorates the formation of Khalsa Panth of warriors under Guru Gobind Singh in 1699.

Codes

(a) Both A and R are true and R is the correct explanation of A
(b) Both A and R are true, but R is not the correct explanation of A
(c) A is true, but R is false
(d) A is false, but R is true

29. Match the following.

List I	List II
A. Lavani	1. Classical dance of Kerala
B. Garba	2. Folk dance of Gujarat
C. Mohiniyattam	3. Classical dance of Andhra Pradesh
D. Kuchipudi	4. Folk dance of Maharashtra

Codes

	A	B	C	D		A	B	C	D
(a)	2	4	1	3	(b)	1	2	3	4
(c)	4	2	1	3	(d)	3	2	4	1

Darken your choice with HB Pencil

1. ⓐ ⓑ ⓒ ⓓ	6. ⓐ ⓑ ⓒ ⓓ	11. ⓐ ⓑ ⓒ ⓓ	16. ⓐ ⓑ ⓒ ⓓ	21. ⓐ ⓑ ⓒ ⓓ	26. ⓐ ⓑ ⓒ ⓓ
2. ⓐ ⓑ ⓒ ⓓ	7. ⓐ ⓑ ⓒ ⓓ	12. ⓐ ⓑ ⓒ ⓓ	17. ⓐ ⓑ ⓒ ⓓ	22. ⓐ ⓑ ⓒ ⓓ	27. ⓐ ⓑ ⓒ ⓓ
3. ⓐ ⓑ ⓒ ⓓ	8. ⓐ ⓑ ⓒ ⓓ	13. ⓐ ⓑ ⓒ ⓓ	18. ⓐ ⓑ ⓒ ⓓ	23. ⓐ ⓑ ⓒ ⓓ	28. ⓐ ⓑ ⓒ ⓓ
4. ⓐ ⓑ ⓒ ⓓ	9. ⓐ ⓑ ⓒ ⓓ	14. ⓐ ⓑ ⓒ ⓓ	19. ⓐ ⓑ ⓒ ⓓ	24. ⓐ ⓑ ⓒ ⓓ	29. ⓐ ⓑ ⓒ ⓓ
5. ⓐ ⓑ ⓒ ⓓ	10. ⓐ ⓑ ⓒ ⓓ	15. ⓐ ⓑ ⓒ ⓓ	20. ⓐ ⓑ ⓒ ⓓ	25. ⓐ ⓑ ⓒ ⓓ	

Chapter 04

First in India and the World

MCQs 1 Mark Questions

1. Who was the first finance minister of independent India?
(a) Liaquat Ali Khan
(b) RK Shanmukham
(c) John Matthai
(d) CD Deshmukh

2. Who was the first Vice President of India?
(a) Dr Sarvepalli Radhakrishnan
(b) Dr Rajendra Prasad
(c) Pt Jawaharlal Nehru
(d) None of the above

3. What is the name of India's first woman to swim across English channel?
(a) Santosh Yadav (b) Ashapurna Devi
(c) Arati Saha (d) Bachendri Pal

4. Identify who amongst the following was the first Indian to be elected to the British Parliament.
(a) Badruddin Tyabji
(b) Dadabhai Naoroji
(c) Pherozeshah Mehta
(d) Surendranath Banerjee

5. Name the Indian social reformer, who is popularly known as the first female teacher of India.
(a) Sarojini Naidu (b) Kiran Bedi
(c) Rani Lakshmi Bai (d) Savitribai Phule

6. Identify the incorrectly matched pair.

(a) First Education Minister of Free India	–	Maulana Abul Kalam Azad
(b) First President of India	–	Dr Rajendra Prasad
(c) First Speaker of Lok Sabha	–	Dr S Radhakrishnan
(d) India's First Home Minister	–	Sardar Vallabhbhai Patel

7. Identify the person who was the first and the last Indian Governor General of free India.
(a) Rajendra Prasaad
(b) Lord Mountbatten
(c) C Rajagopalachari
(d) Lord William Bentinck

8. Identify the name of personality who become the first female defence minister of India.
(a) Amrita Kaur (b) Nirmala Sitharaman
(c) Indira Gandhi (d) Sushma Swaraj

9. Who was the first Indian and last Muslim woman ruler of India?
(a) Razia Sultan (b) Noor Jahan
(c) Fatima Bibi (d) Begum Hazrat Mahal

10. Who was the first woman in India to climb Mount Everest?
(a) Premlata Agarwal (b) Bachendri Pal
(c) Santosh Yadav (d) Arunima Sinha

11. .... was the first Indian to clear the Indian Civil Service.
(a) Satyendranath Tagore
(b) RN Banerjee
(c) Subhash Chandra Bose
(d) Rabindranath Tagore

12. Name the Indian freedom fighter of India who became the first woman Chief Minister of Indian state.
(a) Kamini Roy (b) Sucheta Kriplani
(c) Kiran Bedi (d) Sushma Chawla

13. Which among the following is the first Secretory General of the United Nations?
(a) Kofi Annan (b) Autonio Guterres
(c) Ban Ki-Moon (d) Trygve Lie

14. Identify the incorrectly matched pair.

	First in India		Visitor, travellers
(a)	First Foreign Visitor	–	Megasthenes
(b)	First Muslim Visitor	–	Al-Biruni
(c)	First Chinese Pilgrim	–	Fa-hein
(d)	First European Visitor	–	Ibn battuta

15. Which one of the following is India's first indigenous nuclear sub-marine?
(a) INS Tihayu (b) INS Astradharini
(c) INS Virat (d) INS Arihant

16. Complete the given analogy.
1st India missile : Prithvi : : 1st Medium range missile : ?
(a) Agni (b) Nag
(c) Akash (d) Trishul

17. Which among the following is the first satellite of India?
(a) Aryabhatta (b) Apsara
(c) Bhaskara (d) Sputnik

18. Name the first country to launch the satellite into space.
(a) India (b) Russia
(c) Japan (d) America

19. Who was the first Indian to receive the Bharat Ratna Award?
(a) Jawaharlal Nehru (b) CV Raman
(c) Rajendra Prasad (d) None of these

20. Which among the following was the first Indian to receive Nobel Prize in Economics?
(a) Amartya Sen (b) Bibek Debroy
(c) Dadabhai Naoroji (d) Manmohan Singh

21. Name the person who was the first Indian to receive Magsaysay Award.
(a) Mahatma Gandhi
(b) Sardar Vallabhbhai Patel
(c) Acharya Vinoba Bhave
(d) Sarojini Naid

MCQs 2 Marks Questions

22. Read the given statements and identifies which ones are true (T) and which ones are false (F).
I. Santosh Yadav was the first woman to climb Mount Everest twice.
II. Sir Osborne Smith was the first RBI Governor of India.
III. Annie Besant was the first woman President of INC.
IV. Reita Faria Powell is the first woman to become 'Miss World'.

Codes

	I	II	III	IV		I	II	III	IV
(a)	T	F	F	T	(b)	T	T	F	T
(c)	F	F	T	T	(d)	T	T	T	T

23. Identify the famous personality with the help of the information given below.
- She was popularly known as Bharatiya Kokila.
- She become the first female Governor of India.

(a) Indira Gandhi (b) Meira Kumar
(c) Sarojini Naidu (d) Sonia Gandhi

24. Read the following statements and select the correct option.

I. The first female Prime Minister in the world was Sirimavo Bandaranaike.

II. Benazir Bhutto became the first female Prime Minister of a Muslim country.

Codes

(a) Both I and II (b) Only II

(c) Only I (d) Neither I nor II

25. Identify among the states marked on the map which becomes India's first fully organic state.

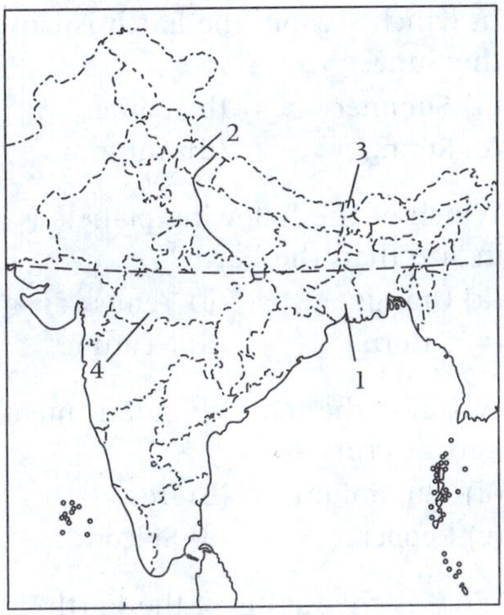

(a) 1 (b) 2

(c) 3 (d) 4

26. Which of the following statements is/are correct and select the correct option.

I. China was the first country to issue paper currency in 806 AD.

II. The first bank note was issued by the Bank of Japan in 1885.

Codes

(a) Only I (b) Only II

(c) Both I and II (d) Neither I nor II

27. There are two statements marked as Assertion (A) and Reason (R). Mark your answer as per the codes given below.

Assertion (A) Russia is the first country to launch an artificial satellite in the space.

Reason (R) It was launched into an elliptical low Earth orbit as part of the Soviet space programme.

Codes

(a) Both A and R are true and R is the correct explanation of A

(b) Both A and R are true, but R is not the correct explanation of A

(c) A is true, but R is false

(d) A is false, but R is true

28. Match the following.

	List I (First in India)		List II (Personality)
A.	First woman to get Noble Prize	1.	Vijaya Lakshmi Pandit
B.	First woman ambassador at United Nations	2.	Kalpana Chawla
C.	First woman to go to the space	3.	Sushmita Sen
D.	First women to become 'Miss Universe'	4.	Mother Teresa

Codes

	A	B	C	D		A	B	C	D
(a)	4	3	2	1	(b)	2	1	4	3
(c)	1	2	4	3	(d)	4	1	2	3

Darken your choice with HB Pencil

1.	ⓐ ⓑ ⓒ ⓓ	6.	ⓐ ⓑ ⓒ ⓓ	11.	ⓐ ⓑ ⓒ ⓓ	16.	ⓐ ⓑ ⓒ ⓓ	21.	ⓐ ⓑ ⓒ ⓓ	26.	ⓐ ⓑ ⓒ ⓓ
2.	ⓐ ⓑ ⓒ ⓓ	7.	ⓐ ⓑ ⓒ ⓓ	12.	ⓐ ⓑ ⓒ ⓓ	17.	ⓐ ⓑ ⓒ ⓓ	22.	ⓐ ⓑ ⓒ ⓓ	27.	ⓐ ⓑ ⓒ ⓓ
3.	ⓐ ⓑ ⓒ ⓓ	8.	ⓐ ⓑ ⓒ ⓓ	13.	ⓐ ⓑ ⓒ ⓓ	18.	ⓐ ⓑ ⓒ ⓓ	23.	ⓐ ⓑ ⓒ ⓓ	28.	ⓐ ⓑ ⓒ ⓓ
4.	ⓐ ⓑ ⓒ ⓓ	9.	ⓐ ⓑ ⓒ ⓓ	14.	ⓐ ⓑ ⓒ ⓓ	19.	ⓐ ⓑ ⓒ ⓓ	24.	ⓐ ⓑ ⓒ ⓓ		
5.	ⓐ ⓑ ⓒ ⓓ	10.	ⓐ ⓑ ⓒ ⓓ	15.	ⓐ ⓑ ⓒ ⓓ	20.	ⓐ ⓑ ⓒ ⓓ	25.	ⓐ ⓑ ⓒ ⓓ		

Chapter 05

Know Your Earth

MCQs 1 Mark Questions

1. The Earth is the .... largest planet in the Solar System.
(a) first (b) fifth
(c) third (d) fourth

2. What is the average density of the Earth?
(a) 2.3 g/cm^3 (b) 3.34 g/cm^3
(c) 5.5 g/cm^3 (d) 1.41 g/cm^3

3. Which among the following rocks present in Earth contain fossils?
(a) Igneous rocks
(b) Metamorphic rocks
(c) Sedimentary rocks
(d) All of the above

4. Which is not a part of the Earth's interior?
(a) Mantle (b) Core
(c) Lithosphere (d) Crust

5. On which date the Earth has the smallest day and longest night in India?
(a) 22nd December (b) 21st June
(c) 1st April (d) 30th April

6. What is the name of outermost solid part of the Earth?
(a) Core (b) Crust
(c) Mantle (d) Magma

7. In which season, the Earth is closest to the Sun?
(a) Summer (b) Winter
(c) Spring (d) Autumn

8. Which of the following planets is smaller in size than the Earth?
(a) Uranus (b) Venus
(c) Saturn (d) Neptune

9. Which is the most abundant metal in the Earth's crust ?
(a) Aluminium (b) Iron
(c) Copper (d) Silicon

10. What is the radius of the Earth?
(a) 5999 km
(b) 6371 km
(c) 6990 km
(d) 9066 km

11. What is the time taken by light to travel from the Sun to the Earth?
(a) 8 minutes
(b) 15 minutes
(c) 3 minutes
(d) 10 minutes

12. Which among the following is a point in the Earth's orbit when it is farthest to the Sun?
(a) Perigee (b) Aphelion
(c) Perihelion (d) Apogee

13. Name the elements which are found in the mantle layer of the Earth.
(a) Silicon and Alumina
(b) Silicon and Magnesium
(c) Nickel and Iron
(d) Iron and Silicon

14. Identify the various layers of the Earth in chronological order from interior to the outermost layer.
(a) Inner core, outer core, mantle, crust
(b) Inner core, outer core, crust, mantle
(c) Crust, mantle, outer core, inner core
(d) Mantle, crust, outer core, inner core

15. The upper portion of the mantle is called ....
(a) lithosphere (b) asthenosphere
(c) solid mantle (d) liquid mantle

16. Which among the following stars is nearest to the Earth?
(a) Sun (b) Alpha Centauri
(c) Pole star (d) Chitra

17. What region of the Earth takes up the greatest volume?
(a) Crust (b) Outer core
(c) Inner core (d) Mantle

18. How many times the Sun shines vertically on the equator?
(a) Twice a year
(b) Once a year
(c) For six month
(d) Throughtout the year

19. Identify the correctly matched pairs.
(a) Red Planet – Venus
(b) Ringed planet – Saturn
(c) Brightest planet – Mars
(d) Hottest planet – Mercury

20. What among the following is the most abundant element in the Earth's crust?
(a) Silicon (b) Carbon
(c) Oxygen (d) Calcium

21. Which one of the following is caused by seismic waves on the Earth?
(a) Volcano (b) Tides
(c) Storm (d) Earthquakes

22. The scale used for measuring the intensity of the earthquake is ....
(a) Mercalli scale (b) Richter scale
(c) Seismograph (d) None of these

23. Which of the following is an example of the most explosive type of volcanoes on the Earth?
(a) Shield volcanoes
(b) Composite volcanoes
(c) Cinder cone
(d) Caldera

MCQs 2 Marks Questions

24. Which of the following statements is/are correct regarding planet Venus?
I. It is the hottest planet in our Solar System.
II. The Soviet Union is the first nation to land on the surface of Venus.

Codes
(a) Only I (b) Only II
(c) Both I and II (d) Neither I nor II

25. There are two statements marked as Assertion (A) and Reason (R). Mark your answer as per the codes given below.

Assertion (A) Volcanic eruption is accompanied by earthquakes.

Reason (R) Volcano erupt water vapours and dust particles in the atmosphere.

Codes
(a) Both A and R are true and R is the correct explanation of A
(b) Both A and R are true, but R is not the correct explanation of A
(c) A is true, but R is false
(d) A is false, but R is true

26. Read the following statements and choose the correct option.

I. Lithosphere is made up of the crust and the uppermost solid layer of the Earth.

II. Fossils are remains of dead plants and animals.

Codes

(a) Only I (b) Only II
(c) Both I and II (d) Neither I nor II

27. Match the following.

List I (Planet)	List II (Characteristics)
A. Jupiter	1. Four times the size of the Earth
B. Uranus	2. Second largest planet in the Solar System
C. Saturn	3. Fastest rotation in the Solar System
D. Neptune	4. Farthest and coldest planet

Codes

	A	B	C	D		A	B	C	D
(a)	3	1	2	4	(b)	3	1	4	2
(c)	2	1	3	4	(d)	2	1	4	3

28. Consider the following statements and choose the correct option.

I. The gravitational force of the Earth is greatest near poles.

II. The Asthenosphere is the lower position of the mantle.

III. The highest temperature is found inside the core of the Earth.

Codes

(a) Both I and II (b) Both II and III
(c) Both I and III (d) I, II and III

29. Read the given statements and identifies which ones are true (T) and which ones are false (F).

I. Meteoroids are small fragments of rock and metal travelling through the space.

II. Comets are smallest units of the cosmic bodies which is made up of frozen gas, rocky and dusts.

III. Asteroids are rocky bodies, which lies between the orbits of Mars and Jupiter.

Codes

	I	II	III		I	II	III
(a)	F	F	T	(b)	T	T	F
(c)	T	T	T	(d)	F	T	F

30. Identify the event with the help of the information given below.

- It happens when the Moon passes between the Sun and the Earth.
- The Moon blocks the light of the Sun from reaching the Earth's surface and cast a shadow on it.

(a) Solar Eclipse
(b) Lunar Eclipse
(c) Partial Lunar Eclipse
(d) Penumbral Lunar Eclipse

Darken your choice with HB Pencil

1. ⓐ ⓑ ⓒ ⓓ	6. ⓐ ⓑ ⓒ ⓓ	11. ⓐ ⓑ ⓒ ⓓ	16. ⓐ ⓑ ⓒ ⓓ	21. ⓐ ⓑ ⓒ ⓓ	26. ⓐ ⓑ ⓒ ⓓ
2. ⓐ ⓑ ⓒ ⓓ	7. ⓐ ⓑ ⓒ ⓓ	12. ⓐ ⓑ ⓒ ⓓ	17. ⓐ ⓑ ⓒ ⓓ	22. ⓐ ⓑ ⓒ ⓓ	27. ⓐ ⓑ ⓒ ⓓ
3. ⓐ ⓑ ⓒ ⓓ	8. ⓐ ⓑ ⓒ ⓓ	13. ⓐ ⓑ ⓒ ⓓ	18. ⓐ ⓑ ⓒ ⓓ	23. ⓐ ⓑ ⓒ ⓓ	28. ⓐ ⓑ ⓒ ⓓ
4. ⓐ ⓑ ⓒ ⓓ	9. ⓐ ⓑ ⓒ ⓓ	14. ⓐ ⓑ ⓒ ⓓ	19. ⓐ ⓑ ⓒ ⓓ	24. ⓐ ⓑ ⓒ ⓓ	29. ⓐ ⓑ ⓒ ⓓ
5. ⓐ ⓑ ⓒ ⓓ	10. ⓐ ⓑ ⓒ ⓓ	15. ⓐ ⓑ ⓒ ⓓ	20. ⓐ ⓑ ⓒ ⓓ	25. ⓐ ⓑ ⓒ ⓓ	30. ⓐ ⓑ ⓒ ⓓ

Chapter 06

Continents and Oceans

MCQs 1 Mark Questions

1. Which of the following is the largest continent in the world?
(a) Asia (b) Australia
(c) South America (d) North America

2. Identify the continent of the world that does not have a desert.
(a) Australia (b) Europe
(c) North America (d) Asia

3. The continent through which both the Tropic of Cancer and the Tropic of Capricorn passes is …… .
(a) Africa (b) Asia
(c) North America (d) South America

4. Pick the odd one out.
(a) Antarctica (b) Africa
(c) Europe (d) Russia

5. Which among the following continents is called the white continent?
(a) Antarctica
(b) Australia
(c) North America
(d) South America

6. The highest mountain of the world 'Mount Everest' is located in which continent?
(a) Africa (b) Asia
(c) North America (d) Europe

7. Identify the name of the continent that form a mirror image of each other.
(a) Africa and South America
(b) Europe and Asia
(c) North America and South America
(d) Asia and Africa

8. Name the personality who gave the Plate Tectonics Theory.
(a) Harry Hammond Hess
(b) Alfred Wegener
(c) W Jason Morgan
(d) John Tuzo Wilson

9. Which is the second largest continent in the world?
(a) Asia (b) Europe
(c) Africa (d) South America

10. In which continent is the highest waterfall 'Angel falls' located?
(a) Asia (b) Africa
(c) North America (d) South America

11. …………….. continent has six months of daylight and six months of darkness.
(a) Australia (b) Antarctica
(c) Europe (d) Asia

12. Which one of the following is the smallest continent?
(a) Asia (b) Antarctica
(c) Europe (d) Australia

13. Which one of the following seas separated Africa from Asia?
(a) Mediterranean Sea
(b) Black Sea
(c) Baltic Sea
(d) Red Sea

14. About how much position of the Earth is covered with water?
(a) Three-fourth (b) One-half
(c) Two-third (d) Three-fifth

15. Which of the following oceans is 'S' shaped?
(a) Pacific Ocean (b) Arctic Ocean
(c) Indian Ocean (d) Atlantic Ocean

16. Which of the following canals form the boundary between North America and South America?
(a) Panama Canal (b) Suez Canal
(c) Volga-Don Canal (d) The Grand Canal

17. Name the world's largest desert of the continent of Africa.
(a) Kalahari Desert
(b) Sahara Desert
(c) Namib Desert
(d) Guban Desert

18. What is the name of the ocean between North America and Asia?
(a) Pacific Ocean (b) Atlantic Ocean
(c) Indian Ocean (d) Arctic Ocean

19. The largest amount of fresh water on our planet is in ....
(a) river
(b) lakes and streams
(c) glaciers and mountains
(d) underground water

20. Which continent is known as the peninsula of peninsulas?
(a) Asia (b) Europe
(c) Australia (d) South America

21. Which of the following continents has the maximum number of country?
(a) North America (b) South America
(c) Africa (d) Asia

22. Identify the name of longest river in Asia.
(a) Yangtze River (b) Ganga River
(c) Yellow River (d) Mekong River

23. Name the continent in which the Amazon Basin is located.
(a) North America (b) South America
(c) Australia (d) Africa

24. Complete the given analogy.
Borneo Island : Pacific Ocean : : Green land : ?
(a) North Atlantic (b) Arctic Ocean
(c) Both (a) and (b) (d) Neither (a) nor (b)

MCQs 2 Marks Questions

25. Consider the following statements about continent and select the correct option.
I. The Australia is the only continent without an active volcano.
II. The continent 'Asia' shares its West border with Pacific Ocean.
III. The South Pole lies almost at the centre of Antarctica.

Codes
(a) I and II (b) II and III
(c) I and III (d) I, II and III

26. Read the given statements and identifies which ones are true (T) and which ones are false (F).
I. The Mariana Trench is the deepest point on the Earth's surface, located in the Pacific Ocean.
II. South America is the continent between the Atlantic and Pacific Ocean.

III. Red Sea separates the continent of Asia and Africa.

Codes

	I	II	III		I	II	III
(a)	T	T	T	(b)	F	F	F
(c)	T	T	F	(d)	F	F	T

27. Match the following.

List I (Continent)	**List II** (Highest Peak)
A. Africa	1. Mount Mc Kinely
B. Europe	2. Mount Kilimanjaro
C. South America	3. Mount Elbrus
D. North America	4. Mount Aconcagua

Codes

	A	B	C	D		A	B	C	D
(a)	3	2	4	1	(b)	2	3	4	1
(c)	2	3	1	4	(d)	3	2	1	4

28. Identify the strait with the help of the information given below.

- It is a strait between the Pacific and Arctic Ocean.
- It is a strait that separates Asia from North America.

(a) Strait of Gibralter (b) Berring Strait
(c) Strait of Malacca (d) Palk Strait

29. Consider the following statements and select the correct option.

I. Lake superior is the largest fresh water lake of the world, located in the North America.

II. Lake Baikal is the deepest lake in the world, located in the African continent.

Codes

(a) Only I (b) Only II
(c) Both I and II (d) Neither I nor II

30. There are two statements marked as Assertion (A) and Reason (R). Mark your answer as per the codes given below.

Assertion (A) Antarctica is the southernmost and fifth largest continent in the world.

Reason (R) It contains 90 per cent of all of the ice on the Earth.

Codes

(a) Both A and R are true, and R is the correct explanation of A
(b) Both A and R are true, but R is not the correct explanation of A
(c) A is true, but R is false
(d) R is true, but A is false

31. Identify the ocean marked as A on the world map given below, which is the second largest of the world's five oceans.

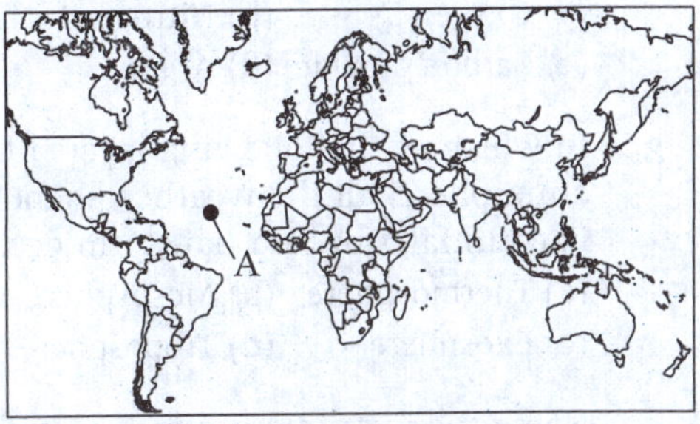

(a) Pacific Ocean (b) Atlantic Ocean
(c) Indian Ocean (d) Arctic Ocean

Darken your choice with HB Pencil

1. ⓐ ⓑ ⓒ ⓓ	7. ⓐ ⓑ ⓒ ⓓ	13. ⓐ ⓑ ⓒ ⓓ	19. ⓐ ⓑ ⓒ ⓓ	25. ⓐ ⓑ ⓒ ⓓ	31. ⓐ ⓑ ⓒ ⓓ
2. ⓐ ⓑ ⓒ ⓓ	8. ⓐ ⓑ ⓒ ⓓ	14. ⓐ ⓑ ⓒ ⓓ	20. ⓐ ⓑ ⓒ ⓓ	26. ⓐ ⓑ ⓒ ⓓ	
3. ⓐ ⓑ ⓒ ⓓ	9. ⓐ ⓑ ⓒ ⓓ	15. ⓐ ⓑ ⓒ ⓓ	21. ⓐ ⓑ ⓒ ⓓ	27. ⓐ ⓑ ⓒ ⓓ	
4. ⓐ ⓑ ⓒ ⓓ	10. ⓐ ⓑ ⓒ ⓓ	16. ⓐ ⓑ ⓒ ⓓ	22. ⓐ ⓑ ⓒ ⓓ	28. ⓐ ⓑ ⓒ ⓓ	
5. ⓐ ⓑ ⓒ ⓓ	11. ⓐ ⓑ ⓒ ⓓ	17. ⓐ ⓑ ⓒ ⓓ	23. ⓐ ⓑ ⓒ ⓓ	29. ⓐ ⓑ ⓒ ⓓ	
6. ⓐ ⓑ ⓒ ⓓ	12. ⓐ ⓑ ⓒ ⓓ	18. ⓐ ⓑ ⓒ ⓓ	24. ⓐ ⓑ ⓒ ⓓ	30. ⓐ ⓑ ⓒ ⓓ	

Chapter 07

Components of Life-Air and Water

MCQs 1 Mark Questions

1. What is the composition of the nitrogen gas in the atmosphere?
(a) 78% (b) 21%
(c) 65% (d) 55%

2. Which of the following gases released in the atmosphere creates a green house effect trapping the heat?
(a) Oxygen (b) Nitrogen
(c) Carbon dioxide (d) Argon

3. In which of the following layers of atmosphere, all the weather phenomena like rainfall, fog and hailstorm occur?
(a) Thermosphere (b) Mesosphere
(c) Exosphere (d) Troposphere

4. Name the instrument which is used to measure the atmospheric pressure.
(a) Barometer
(b) Rain gauge
(c) Altimeter
(d) Hygrometer

5. Name the uppermost layer of the atmosphere.
(a) Troposphere (b) Exosphere
(c) Thermosphere (d) Stratosphere

6. Which layer of the atmosphere is free from clouds?
(a) Mesosphere (b) Troposphere
(c) Stratosphere (d) Exosphere

7. Which layer of the atmosphere contains the Ozone that is responsible for the absorption of ultraviolet (UV) radiation?
(a) Stratosphere (b) Troposphere
(c) Mesosphere (d) Thermosphere

8. Complete the given analogy.
Coldest layer : Mesosphere : : Hottest layer : ?
(a) Stratosphere
(b) Thermosphere
(c) Mesosphere
(d) Troposphere

9. Which one of the following gases is not a greenhouse gas?
(a) Carbon dioxide
(b) Methane
(c) Oxygen
(d) Nitrous oxide

10. Name the instrument which is used to measure temperature.
(a) Hydrometer (b) Thermometer
(c) Wind vane (d) Rain gauge

11. Identify the correct chronology of the layers of the atmosphere.
(a) Troposphere, Stratosphere, Mesosphere,, Thermosphere, Exosphere
(b) Troposphere, Stratosphere, Thermosphere, Mesosphere, Exosphere
(c) Troposphere, Mesosphere, Stratosphere, Thermosphere, Exosphere
(d) Troposphere, Thermosphere, Exosphere, Mesosphere

12. Which one of the following is not a type of rainfall?
(a) Convectional rainfall
(b) Cyclonic rainfall
(c) Cloudy rainfall
(d) Orographic rainfall

13. Identify instrument which is used for measuring rainfall.
(a) Barometer (b) Rain gauge
(c) Hydrometer (d) Ammeter

14. The rhythmic rise and fall of ocean water twice in a day is called ....
(a) wave (b) current
(c) tides (d) tsunami

15. Which one of the following has the least percentage of water present on the Earth?
(a) Ocean water (b) Ice caps
(c) Ground water (d) Fresh water

16. During the full Moon and new Moon, the Sun, the Moon and the Earth are in the same line and the tides are highest. These tides are called ....
(a) mixed tides (b) diurnal tides
(c) spring tides (d) neap tides

17. Which element of weather is measured in degree celsius?
(a) Temperature (b) Pressure
(c) Gravity (d) Wind

18. Which of the following factors affect the movement of ocean water?
(a) Temperature
(b) Warm and cold current
(c) The gravitational pull of Moon and Sun
(d) All of the above

19. Identify the factor(s) affecting the height of the waves.
(a) Earthquake
(b) Volcanic eruption
(c) Underwater landslide
(d) All of the above

20. The process by which water continually changes its form and circulates between oceans, atmosphere and land is called ....
(a) water cycle (b) ocean currents
(c) tides (d) rain water

21. Which one of the following are the ways to conserve water?
(a) Ground water harvesting
(b) Storing rain water from roof tops
(c) Both (a) and (b)
(d) By using hand pumps

22. Identify the incorrectly matched pair.

	Atmospheric layers		Height
(a)	Troposphere	–	15 km
(b)	Stratosphere	–	15-50 km
(c)	Mesosphere	–	50-80 km
(d)	Ionosphere	–	Below 50 km

23. Which layer of atmosphere is used for telecommunication?
(a) Troposphere (b) Thermosphere
(c) Stratosphere (d) Ionosphere

24. Identify the major source(s) of fresh water on the Earth.
(a) Glaciers
(b) Stream and rivers
(c) Lakes, ponds and wetlands
(d) All of the above

25. The actual amount of water vapour present in the atmosphere is known as ....

(a) relative humidity (b) absolute humidity
(c) specific humidity (d) condensation

26. The process of conversion of water vapour into water is called ....

(a) condensation (b) evaporation
(c) precipitation (d) transpiration

27. Name two gases which make up 99 % of the Earth's atmosphere.

(a) Hydrogen and Nitrogen
(b) Hydrogen and Helium
(c) Nitrogen and Oxygen
(d) Carbon dioxide and Helium

28. Which layer of the atmosphere is 8 km above the pole and 18 km high at the equator?

(a) Troposphere (b) Stratosphere
(c) Mesosphere (d) Exosphere

29. Identify the picture and name the phenomenon which is shown in the picture given below.

(a) Oxygen Cycle
(b) Carbon Cycle
(c) Water Cycle
(d) Nitrogen Cycle

30. Radio waves transmitted from the Earth are reflected back by which of the following layers?

(a) Troposphere (b) Stratosphere
(c) Mesosphere (d) Thermosphere

MCQs 2 Marks Questions

31. Read the following statements and select the correct option.

I. Rainwater is consider as the purest form of water.
II. Rain shadow zone means leeward side of the mountain.

Codes

(a) Both I and II (b) Only II
(c) Only I (d) Neither I nor II

32. Consider the following statements and choose the correct option.

I. The trade wind is an example of permanent wind.
II. The monsoon is a seasonal wind of the Indian Ocean and South-East Asia.
III. The air pressure always decrease with the increasing altitude.

Codes

(a) I and II (b) II and III
(c) I and III (d) I, II and III

33. There are two statements marked as Assertion (A) and Reason (R). Mark your answer as per the codes given below.

Assertion (A) The amount of insulation decreases from the equator toward poles.

Reason (R) The Sun rays fall vertically on the equator and slant on the poles.

Codes

(a) Both A and R are true and R is the correct explanation of A
(b) Both A and R are true, but R is not the correct explanation of A
(c) A is true, but R is false
(d) A is false, but R is true

34. Read the given statements and identifies which ones are true (T) and which ones are false (F).

I. Humidity is the amount of water vapour in the air.

II. The permanent wind blows constantly throughout the year in particular direction.

III. The warm and cold current originated near poles.

IV. Waves are formed when winds scrape across the ocean surface.

Codes

	I	II	III	IV		I	II	III	IV
(a)	F	T	T	F	(b)	T	T	F	T
(c)	T	T	T	T	(d)	F	T	F	F

35. Consider the following statements and choose the correct option.

I. Hot air is dense and heavy, and cold air is lighter and expands.

II. Helium and hydrogen float from exosphere into space.

III. Air moves from high pressure to low pressure.

Codes

(a) I and III (b) II and III
(c) I and II (d) I, II and III

36. There are two statements marked as Assertion (A) and Reason (R). Mark your answer as per the codes given below.

Assertion (A) Jet planes flying in the sky leave a white trail behind them.

Reason (R) The moisture from their engine condenses.

Codes

(a) Both A and R are true and R is the correct explanation of A
(b) Both A and R are true, but R is not the correct explanation of A
(c) A is true, but R is false
(d) A is false, but R is true

37. Identify the local winds with the help of the information given below.

- It blows only during a particular period of the day or year in a small area.
- It blows between tiny low and high pressure system.

(a) Sea breeze (b) Trade wind
(c) Monsoon wind (d) None of these

38. Consider the following statements and select the correct option.

I. The rainfall on the Earth is caused by evaporation.

II. Most of the water is available to us as ground water inside the Earth crust.

III. Ocean water is a source of fresh water.

Codes

(a) I and III (b) II and III
(c) I and II (d) I, II and III

39. Match the following.

	List I		List II
A.	Trade Winds	1.	Seasonal wind
B.	Loo	2.	Horizontal movement of air
C.	Monsoon	3.	Permanent wind
D.	Wind	4.	Local wind

Codes

	A	B	C	D		A	B	C	D
(a)	2	3	4	1	(b)	1	2	3	4
(c)	1	3	2	4	(d)	3	2	1	4

Darken your choice with HB Pencil

1.	(a) (b) (c) (d)	8.	(a) (b) (c) (d)	15.	(a) (b) (c) (d)	22.	(a) (b) (c) (d)	29.	(a) (b) (c) (d)	36.	(a) (b) (c) (d)
2.	(a) (b) (c) (d)	9.	(a) (b) (c) (d)	16.	(a) (b) (c) (d)	23.	(a) (b) (c) (d)	30.	(a) (b) (c) (d)	37.	(a) (b) (c) (d)
3.	(a) (b) (c) (d)	10.	(a) (b) (c) (d)	17.	(a) (b) (c) (d)	24.	(a) (b) (c) (d)	31.	(a) (b) (c) (d)	38.	(a) (b) (c) (d)
4.	(a) (b) (c) (d)	11.	(a) (b) (c) (d)	18.	(a) (b) (c) (d)	25.	(a) (b) (c) (d)	32.	(a) (b) (c) (d)	39.	(a) (b) (c) (d)
5.	(a) (b) (c) (d)	12.	(a) (b) (c) (d)	19.	(a) (b) (c) (d)	26.	(a) (b) (c) (d)	33.	(a) (b) (c) (d)		
6.	(a) (b) (c) (d)	13.	(a) (b) (c) (d)	20.	(a) (b) (c) (d)	27.	(a) (b) (c) (d)	34.	(a) (b) (c) (d)		
7.	(a) (b) (c) (d)	14.	(a) (b) (c) (d)	21.	(a) (b) (c) (d)	28.	(a) (b) (c) (d)	35.	(a) (b) (c) (d)		

Chapter 08

Physical Features of India

MCQs 1 Mark Questions

1. India is situated in which continent?
(a) North America (b) Europe
(c) Asia (d) Africa

2. What is the length of India from North to South?
(a) 2,415 km (b) 3,315 km
(c) 3,214 km (d) 2,715 km

3. Name the Southern point of India's mainland.
(a) Tamil Nadu (b) Goa
(c) Kanyakumari (d) Kerala

4. India is located in which hemisphere?
(a) Northern Hemisphere
(b) Southern Hemisphere
(c) North-Eastern Hemisphere
(d) None of the above

5. Name the longest river of our country India.
(a) Brahmaputra (b) Ganga
(c) Godavari (d) Kaveri

6. The Pir Panjal pass is located in province of India.
(a) Jammu and Kashmir
(b) Sikkim
(c) Himachal Pradesh
(d) Uttarakhand State

7. Name the geographical term which is related to a body of land surrounded by water on three sides.
(a) Peninsula (b) Gulf
(c) Strait (d) Island

8. Which among the following passes link Srinagar to Leh?
(a) Mana Pass (b) Rohtas Pass
(c) Nathula Pass (d) Zoji La Pass

9. Which is the Easternmost longitude of India?
(a) 97° 25′ E (b) 77° 6′ E
(c) 68° 7′ E (d) 82° 32′ E

10. Name the country which does not share land boundary with India.
(a) Bhutan (b) Bangladesh
(c) Tajikistan (d) Nepal

11. Which of the following is called the Southernmost Himalayas?
(a) Shivalik (b) Himadri
(c) Himachal (d) None of these

12. What is the another name of Sahyadris?
(a) Aravalli
(b) Western Ghats
(c) Himadri
(d) None of the above

13. Where does the Palk Strait lies?
(a) Sri Lanka and Maldives
(b) India and Sri Lanka
(c) India and Maldives
(d) Both (a) and (b)

14. Which of the following is the popular name of the Indian islands in the Arabian Sea?
(a) Andaman and Nicobar Islands
(b) Lakshadweep Islands
(c) Maldives
(d) Both (a) and (b)

15. Which of the following is the oldest mountain range in India?
(a) Aravalli mountains
(b) Western Ghats
(c) Himalayas
(d) Both (a) and (c)

16. What is the length of the coastline in India?
(a) 5,500 km (b) 9,500 km
(c) 4,500 km (d) 7,516 km

17. Name the state of India which has the longest coastline.
(a) Gujarat (b) Karnataka
(c) Tamil Nadu (d) Odisha

18. Which among the following places is known as the Silent Valley of India?
(a) Tamil Nadu (b) Goa
(c) Kerala (d) Leh

19. Complete the given analogy.
West Bengal : East : : ? : West
(a) Andhra Pradesh
(b) Maharashtra
(c) Himachal Pradesh
(d) Tamil Nadu

20. Identify the pair of states which are the Easternmost and Westernmost states of India.
(a) Assam and Gujarat
(b) Assam and Rajasthan
(c) Arunachal Pradesh and Rajasthan
(d) Arunachal Pradesh and Gujarat

21. Which among the following hills are called as Purvanchal?
(a) Mizo Hills
(b) Seshadri Hills
(c) Garudadri Hills
(d) Narayanadri Hills

22. Name the highest waterfall of India.
(a) Kunchikal Falls
(b) Dudhsagar Falls
(c) Jog Falls
(d) Kakolat waterfall

23. Identify the correctly matched pair.

	Mountains/ hills	**State**
(a)	Aravalli range	– Gujarat
(b)	Cardamom Hills	– Odisha
(c)	Zaskar Range	– Kashmir Region
(d)	Vindhya Range	– Uttarakhand

24. Identify the physical feature of India as depicted in the picture given below.

(a) Peninsula (b) Island
(c) Plateau (d) Mountain

MCQs 2 Marks Questions

25. Which one of the following are Himalayan ranges?

I. Himadri II. Himachal

III. Kullu IV. Shivalik

Codes

(a) I and II (b) II and III

(c) I, II and III (d) I, II and IV

26. Match the following.

List I (City)	List II (River)
A. Patna	1. Gomti
B. Lucknow	2. Brahmaputra
C. Guwahati	3. Ganga
D. Nashik	4. Godavari

Codes

	A	B	C	D		A	B	C	D
(a)	3	1	2	4	(b)	2	3	4	1
(c)	1	3	2	4	(d)	2	4	3	1

27. Which of the following statements are incorrect.

I. Kanchenjunga mountain is located in the state of Sikkim.

II. Dal lake is located in Uttarakhand.

III. Itanagar receives highest rainfall in India.

Codes

(a) I and II (b) II and III

(c) I and III (d) I, II and III

28. Consider the following statements and choose the correct option.

I. Jhelum river flows through the state of Himachal Pradesh.

II. Sukhna lake is located at Chandigarh.

Codes

(a) Only I (b) Only II

(c) Both I and II (d) None of these

29. Read the given statements and identifies which ones are true (T) and which ones are false (F).

I. The Himalayas form the highest and rugged mountains in the world.

II. The Mount Everest is the highest peak in the world lying in the Himalayas.

III. The Deccan plateau is one of the most ancient landmasses.

IV. Chilka lake is the largest salt water lake on the Eastern Coast of Odisha.

Codes

	I	II	III	IV		I	II	III	IV
(a)	F	T	T	F	(b)	F	F	F	T
(c)	T	T	T	T	(d)	T	F	F	T

30. Which of the following mountains are not found in India?

I. Kilimanjaro

II. Nanda Devi

III. Fuji

Codes

(a) I and II (b) II and III

(c) I and III (d) None of these

31. Consider the following statements and choose the correct option.

I. Mount Abu hill Station is located in the state of Rajasthan.

II. Surat is located on Tapti river.

Codes

(a) Only I

(b) Only II

(c) Both I and II

(d) None of the above

32. Identify the physical feature of India with the help of the information given below.

- This is a tableland composed of the old crystalline, igneous and metamorphic rocks.

- It was formed due to the breaking and drifting of the Gondwana land and thus, making it a part of the oldest landmass.

(a) Indian Desert (b) Peninsular plateau
(c) Himalayan mountain
(d) Coastal plains

33. Which of the following rivers do not fall in the Bay of Bengal?

I. Narmada II. Tapti
III. Mahanadi IV. Damodar

Codes

(a) I and IV (b) II and III
(c) I and II (d) I, II and III

34. Look at the given map of India and identify the mountain peak which is located in Indian state Sikkim.

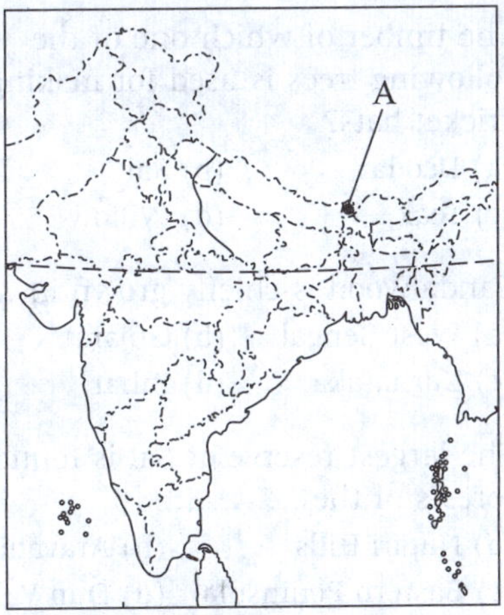

(a) Kanchenjunga peak
(b) K2
(c) Nanda Devi
(d) Nanga Parbat

35. Which of the following regions is /are desert region.

I. Jaisalmer
II. Leh
III. Ran of Kutch

Codes

(a) Only I
(b) I and II
(c) I and III
(d) I, II and III

36. There are two statements marked as Assertion (A) and Reason (R). Mark your answer as per the codes given below.

Assertion (A) The Eastern Ghats are discontinuous and irregular.

Reason (R) Eastern Ghats are cut by rivers flowing into the Bay of Bengal.

Codes

(a) Both A and R is true and R is the correct explanation of A
(b) Both A and R is true, but R is not a correct explanation of A
(c) A is true, but R is false
(d) A is false, but R is true

Darken your choice with HB Pencil

1. ⓐ ⓑ ⓒ ⓓ	7. ⓐ ⓑ ⓒ ⓓ	13. ⓐ ⓑ ⓒ ⓓ	19. ⓐ ⓑ ⓒ ⓓ	25. ⓐ ⓑ ⓒ ⓓ	31. ⓐ ⓑ ⓒ ⓓ
2. ⓐ ⓑ ⓒ ⓓ	8. ⓐ ⓑ ⓒ ⓓ	14. ⓐ ⓑ ⓒ ⓓ	20. ⓐ ⓑ ⓒ ⓓ	26. ⓐ ⓑ ⓒ ⓓ	32. ⓐ ⓑ ⓒ ⓓ
3. ⓐ ⓑ ⓒ ⓓ	9. ⓐ ⓑ ⓒ ⓓ	15. ⓐ ⓑ ⓒ ⓓ	21. ⓐ ⓑ ⓒ ⓓ	27. ⓐ ⓑ ⓒ ⓓ	33. ⓐ ⓑ ⓒ ⓓ
4. ⓐ ⓑ ⓒ ⓓ	10. ⓐ ⓑ ⓒ ⓓ	16. ⓐ ⓑ ⓒ ⓓ	22. ⓐ ⓑ ⓒ ⓓ	28. ⓐ ⓑ ⓒ ⓓ	34. ⓐ ⓑ ⓒ ⓓ
5. ⓐ ⓑ ⓒ ⓓ	11. ⓐ ⓑ ⓒ ⓓ	17. ⓐ ⓑ ⓒ ⓓ	23. ⓐ ⓑ ⓒ ⓓ	29. ⓐ ⓑ ⓒ ⓓ	35. ⓐ ⓑ ⓒ ⓓ
6. ⓐ ⓑ ⓒ ⓓ	12. ⓐ ⓑ ⓒ ⓓ	18. ⓐ ⓑ ⓒ ⓓ	24. ⓐ ⓑ ⓒ ⓓ	30. ⓐ ⓑ ⓒ ⓓ	36. ⓐ ⓑ ⓒ ⓓ

Chapter 09

Natural Vegetation and Wildlife

MCQs 1 Mark Questions

1. Which state is the natural habitat of the Indian lion?
(a) Gujarat (b) West Bengal
(c) Odisha (d) Madhya Pradesh

2. Manas Tiger Reserve is located in …….. .
(a) Tamil Nadu (b) Kerala
(c) Assam (d) Odisha

3. When was 'Project Tiger' launched in India?
(a) 1968 (b) 1973
(c) 1984 (d) 1993

4. Which of the following states is the largest producer of bamboo in India?
(a) Jharkhand (b) Madhya Pradesh
(c) Mizoram (d) Uttarakhand

5. Identify the name of the first national park established in India.
(a) Kanha National Park
(b) Dudhwa National Park
(c) Jim Corbett National Park
(d) None of the above

6. Where are Sundarban Mangroves located?
(a) West Bengal (b) Andhra Pradesh
(c) Karnataka (d) Telangana

7. Which of the following is the largest biosphere reserve in India?
(a) Nilgiri (b) Gulf of Mannar
(c) Sundarbans (d) Nanda Devi

8. The timber of which one of the following trees is used for making cricket bats?
(a) Deodar (b) Sal
(c) Teak (d) Willow

9. Sandalwood is chiefly grown in ……… .
(a) West Bengal (b) Gujarat
(c) Karnataka (d) Bihar

10. The largest reserve of Sal is found in the forests of the ………… .
(a) Nilgiri Hills (b) Aravallis
(c) Eastern Peninsula (d) Dun Valley

11. Which of the following states is dominated by desert vegetation?
(a) West Bengal (b) Bihar
(c) Gujarat (d) Rajasthan

12. Complete the given analogy.
Rajasthan : Camel : ? :: Red Panda
(a) Jammu and Kashmir
(b) Sikkim
(c) Tamil Nadu
(d) Himachal Pradesh

13. In which of the following states is the Gulf of Mannar National Park located?
(a) Jharkhand (b) Tamil Nadu
(c) Chhattisgarh (d) Odisha

14. Which of the following is the national aquatic animal of India ?
(a) Saltwater crocodile
(b) Olive ridley turtle
(c) Gangetic dolphin
(d) Gharial

15. Look at the given picture. Which state of India is the home of the animal shown in the given picture?

(a) Jharkhand (b) Odisha
(c) Sikkim (d) Assam

16. Which among the following is the most prevalent hotspots of biodiversity in India?
(a) Himalayas (b) Western Ghats
(c) Ganges (d) None of these

17. Name the type of tree(s) that is/are found in Tropical Evergreen Forests.
(a) Ebony (b) Mahogany
(c) Rosewood (d) All of these

18. Identify the correctly matched pair.

(a) Sultanpur Bird Sanctuary	–	Rajasthan
(b) Kaziranga National Park	–	Arunachal Pradesh
(c) Ranthambore National Park	–	Rajasthan
(d) Gir National Park	–	Madhya Pradesh

19. Complete the given analogy.
Uttarakhand: Jim Corbett National Park: : Kerala : ?
(a) Periyar National Park
(b) Similipal National Park
(c) Kanha National Park
(d) Chandra Prabha National Park

20. Pench Tiger Reserve is located in which state of India?
(a) Jharkhand (b) Madhya Pradesh
(c) Rajasthan (d) Haryana

21. Bandipur National Park is located in which of the following states?
(a) Andhra Pradesh (b) Rajasthan
(c) Assam (d) Karnataka

MCQs 2 Marks Questions

22. There are two statements marked as Assertion (A) and Reason (R). Mark your answer as per the codes given below.

Assertion (A) The production and farming of fish in Andhra Pradesh are the highest in India.

Reason (R) The Andhra Pradesh is located on the South-Eastern Coast.

Codes
(a) Both A and R are true and R is the correct explanation of A
(b) Both A and R are true, but R is not the correct explanation of A
(c) A is true, but R is false
(d) A is false, but R is true

23. Consider the following statements and choose the correct option.
I. Rajaji National Park is located in Uttarakhand.
II. Kanha National Park is located in Madhya Pradesh.

Codes

(a) Only I
(b) Only II
(c) Both I and II
(d) None of the above

24. Match the following.

	List I (Forest)		List II (Tree)
A.	Tropical Evergreen Forests	1.	Mahogany
B.	Tropical Deciduous Forests	2.	Teak
C.	Tropical Thorn Forests	3.	Acacias
D.	Montane Forests	4.	Deodar

Codes

	A	B	C	D		A	B	C	D
(a)	1	2	3	4	(b)	4	3	2	1
(c)	2	4	1	3	(d)	3	1	4	2

25. Identify the type of forest with the help of the information given below.

- These thick forests occur in the regions near the equator and close to the tropics.
- These regions are hot and receive heavy rainfall throughout the year.

(a) Tropical Deciduous Forests
(b) Coniferous Forests
(c) Evergreen Forests
(d) Mangrove Forests

26. Consider the following statements and choose the correct option.

I. The highest tea producing state in India is Assam.

II. Cactus plant is naturally found in cold desert.

Codes

(a) Only I
(b) Only II
(c) Both I and II
(d) None of the above

27. Consider the following statements and choose the incorrect option.

I. Mosses and Lichens are found in the higher elevations of the Himalayas region.

II. Thorny bushes are found in the desert and rain shadow zone of the Eastern Ghats.

Codes

(a) Only I
(b) Only II
(c) Both I and II
(d) None of the above

28. Read the given statements and identifies which ones are true (T) and which ones are false (F).

I. Gulf of Mannar Marine National Park is located in Tamil Nadu.

II. The Keibul Lamjao National Park is the only floating national park in the world.

III. Mudumalai National Park is famous for it's Tiger Reserve in India.

Codes

	I	II	III		I	II	III
(a)	F	T	F	(b)	F	F	T
(c)	T	T	T	(d)	T	F	F

1. ⓐ ⓑ ⓒ ⓓ	6. ⓐ ⓑ ⓒ ⓓ	11. ⓐ ⓑ ⓒ ⓓ	16. ⓐ ⓑ ⓒ ⓓ	21. ⓐ ⓑ ⓒ ⓓ	26. ⓐ ⓑ ⓒ ⓓ
2. ⓐ ⓑ ⓒ ⓓ	7. ⓐ ⓑ ⓒ ⓓ	12. ⓐ ⓑ ⓒ ⓓ	17. ⓐ ⓑ ⓒ ⓓ	22. ⓐ ⓑ ⓒ ⓓ	27. ⓐ ⓑ ⓒ ⓓ
3. ⓐ ⓑ ⓒ ⓓ	8. ⓐ ⓑ ⓒ ⓓ	13. ⓐ ⓑ ⓒ ⓓ	18. ⓐ ⓑ ⓒ ⓓ	23. ⓐ ⓑ ⓒ ⓓ	28. ⓐ ⓑ ⓒ ⓓ
4. ⓐ ⓑ ⓒ ⓓ	9. ⓐ ⓑ ⓒ ⓓ	14. ⓐ ⓑ ⓒ ⓓ	19. ⓐ ⓑ ⓒ ⓓ	24. ⓐ ⓑ ⓒ ⓓ	
5. ⓐ ⓑ ⓒ ⓓ	10. ⓐ ⓑ ⓒ ⓓ	15. ⓐ ⓑ ⓒ ⓓ	20. ⓐ ⓑ ⓒ ⓓ	25. ⓐ ⓑ ⓒ ⓓ	

Chapter 10

Transport and Communication

MCQs 1 Mark Questions

1. Which of the following is a tidal port?
(a) Visakhapatnam (b) Kandla
(c) Tuticorin (d) None of these

2. Prayagraj–Haldia Waterway is also known as ....
(a) National Waterway-2
(b) National Waterway-4
(c) National Waterway-1
(d) National Waterway-3

3. In which state is the Mormugao Port located?
(a) Goa (b) Gujarat
(c) Maharashtra (d) Karnataka

4. The highest railway station in India is located in the state of ....
(a) Sikkim (b) Uttarakhand
(c) West Bengal (d) Nagaland

5. The following traffic sign shown in the picture given below is used to indicate ....

(a) cross-road
(b) pedestrian crossing
(c) railway crossing
(d) narrow bridge

6. Which is the cheapest mode of transport for long distance?
(a) Road (b) Rail
(c) Air (d) Water

7. Which among the following is the longest rail route in India?
(a) Kashmir to Bengaluru
(b) Dibrugarh to Kanyakumari
(c) Mizoram to Gujarat
(d) Maharashtra to Manipur

8. Which of the following is the smallest national highway by length in India?
(a) NH-3 (b) NH-118
(c) NH-50 (d) NH-9

9. When did the first passenger train start in India?
(a) 1920 (b) 1856
(c) 1853 (d) 1959

10. Longest railway platform in India is located in which state?
(a) Odisha (b) Maharashtra
(c) Karnataka (d) Uttar Pradesh

11. Which among the following is the artificial port of India?
(a) Kandla (b) Mangalore
(c) Haldia (d) Chennai

12. Paradip is located in the state of ....
(a) Kerala (b) Maharashtra
(c) Andhra Pradesh (d) Odisha

13. The 'Grand Trunk Road' connects which of the following two cities?
(a) Kolkata and Mumbai
(b) Delhi and Chennai
(c) Kolkata and Amritsar
(d) Tirupati and Ludhiana

14. Identify National Highway which connects the four metro cities of India that are Delhi, Mumbai, Kolkata and Chennai.
(a) National Highway-44
(b) National Highway-47A
(c) Golden Quadrilateral (GQ)
(d) North-South Corridor of NHDP

15. The headquarters of Metro Railway Zone is located in ....
(a) New Delhi (b) Mumbai
(c) Kolkata (d) Chennai

Which of the following is India's fastest train?
(a) Rajdhani Express
(b) Vande Bharat Express
(c) Sampurna Kranti
(d) Shatabdi Express

17. Which of the following is not the mass media ?
(a) Telephone (b) Radio
(c) Newspaper (d) Television

18. .... can give messages and information to a number of people at the same time.
(a) Postcard (b) Newspaper
(c) Telephone (d) Letters

19. Identify the incorrectly matched pair.
(a) Radio – Audio media
(b) TV – Audio-visual media
(c) Newspaper – Print Media
(d) Magazine – Audio Media

MCQs 2 Marks Questions

20. Match the following.

	List I (Railway zone)		List II (Headquarters)
A.	Central Railway	1.	Mumbai
B.	Northern Railway	2.	Gorakhpur
C.	North-Eastern Railway	3.	Delhi
D.	North-East Frontier Railway	4.	Guwahati

Codes

	A	B	C	D		A	B	C	D
(a)	1	3	2	4	(b)	2	3	4	1
(c)	1	2	3	4	(d)	3	1	2	4

21. In which of the following places you can see boats being used as mode of transport?
I. Kashmir
II. Kerala
III. Sikkim

Codes
(a) Only I (b) Only II
(c) I and II (d) I and III

22. There are two statements marked as Assertion (A) and Reason (R). Mark your answer as per the codes given below.

Assertion (A) Vallam which is a small or large wooden boat, is used in Kerala as a means of transport by people to travel from one place to another.

Reason (R) Kerala is characterised by longest backwater in India.

Codes

(a) Both A and R are true and R is the correct explanation of A
(b) Both A and R are true, but R is not the correct explanation of A
(c) A is true, but R is false
(d) A is false, but R is true

23. Which of the following statements are incorrect.

I. Mumbai Port is India's largest port by size and shipping traffic.
II. National Highway-1 in India runs between the Union Territories of Jammu and Kashmir and Ladakh.
III. Karnataka has the highest number of airports in India.

Codes

(a) I and II (b) II and III
(c) I and III (d) I, II and III

24. Consider the following statements and choose the correct option.

I. National Highway connects major cities and towns in the countries.
II. India rank first in terms of road network in the world.

Codes

(a) Only I (b) Only II
(c) Both I and II (d) None of these

25. Consider the following statements and choose the correct option.

I. The National Highway is maintained by the National Highway Authority of India.
II. Rural roads are 80 per cent of total road length in India.

Codes

(a) Only I
(b) Only II
(c) Both I and II
(d) None of the above

26. Identify the mode of transport with the help of the information given below.

- These modes of transport are the primary mode of transport for passengers and goods.
- It makes it possible to conduct many activities like business, sightseeing and pilgrimage along with transportation of goods over longer distances.

(a) Roadways (b) Railways
(c) Airways (d) Waterways

27. Read the given statements and identifies which ones are true (T) and which ones are false (F).

I. Indian railways system is the largest in the world.
II. The Northern plain of India has higher East-West railway connectivity than the North-South railway connectivity.
III. Western Railway Zone is the largest railway zone of the Indian railways.

Codes

	I	II	III
(a)	T	F	F
(b)	F	T	T
(c)	T	T	F
(d)	F	F	T

Darken your choice with HB Pencil

1.	ⓐ ⓑ ⓒ ⓓ	6.	ⓐ ⓑ ⓒ ⓓ	11.	ⓐ ⓑ ⓒ ⓓ	16.	ⓐ ⓑ ⓒ ⓓ	21.	ⓐ ⓑ ⓒ ⓓ	26.	ⓐ ⓑ ⓒ ⓓ
2.	ⓐ ⓑ ⓒ ⓓ	7.	ⓐ ⓑ ⓒ ⓓ	12.	ⓐ ⓑ ⓒ ⓓ	17.	ⓐ ⓑ ⓒ ⓓ	22.	ⓐ ⓑ ⓒ ⓓ	27.	ⓐ ⓑ ⓒ ⓓ
3.	ⓐ ⓑ ⓒ ⓓ	8.	ⓐ ⓑ ⓒ ⓓ	13.	ⓐ ⓑ ⓒ ⓓ	18.	ⓐ ⓑ ⓒ ⓓ	23.	ⓐ ⓑ ⓒ ⓓ		
4.	ⓐ ⓑ ⓒ ⓓ	9.	ⓐ ⓑ ⓒ ⓓ	14.	ⓐ ⓑ ⓒ ⓓ	19.	ⓐ ⓑ ⓒ ⓓ	24.	ⓐ ⓑ ⓒ ⓓ		
5.	ⓐ ⓑ ⓒ ⓓ	10.	ⓐ ⓑ ⓒ ⓓ	15.	ⓐ ⓑ ⓒ ⓓ	20.	ⓐ ⓑ ⓒ ⓓ	25.	ⓐ ⓑ ⓒ ⓓ		

Chapter 11

Constitution of India

MCQs 1 Mark Questions

1. Constitution of India was formed by ....
(a) Constituent Assembly
(b) Parliament of India
(c) Law Ministry of Central Government
(d) British Government

2. Who was elected as the first President of the Constituent Assembly?
(a) Dr Rajendra Prasad
(b) Jawaharlal Nehru
(c) Mahatma Gandhi
(d) Dr BR Ambedkar

3. Which among the following proposed the Objective Resolution to the Constitution of India?
(a) Mahatma Gandhi (b) BR Ambedkar
(c) Jawaharlal Nehru (d) Rajendra Prasad

4. Who was the Chairman of the Drafting Committee of the Constituent Assembly?
(a) Dr Rajendra Prasad
(b) Sardar Vallabhbhai Patel
(c) Dr BR Ambedkar
(d) Jawaharlal Nehru

5. The Constitution of India was adopted on ....
(a) 15th August, 1947
(b) 26th January, 1950
(c) 26th November, 1949
(d) 15th August, 1950

6. How much time was taken by Constituent Assembly to write the Constitution?
(a) 2 years, 11 months and 7 days
(b) 2 years, 11 months and 18 days
(c) 3 years, 11 months and 7 days
(d) 3 years, 11 months and 17 days

7. Which of the following is known as the 'Magna Carta' of the Constitution?
(a) Fundamental Rights
(b) Preamble
(c) Fundamental Duties
(d) DPSP

8. Who among the following acts as a Chairman of Rajya Sabha?
(a) President
(b) Vice-President
(c) Prime Minister
(d) Speaker of Lok Sabha

9. Complete the given analogy.
India : Parliamentary System : : America :
(a) Democratic System
(b) Republican System
(c) Presidential System
(d) Authoritarian System

10. Fundamental Duties refer to ....
(a) the duties that are to be expected by the citizen.
(b) the duties to be performed by the states.
(c) duties performed by the Judiciary.
(d) None of the above

11. The words added to the Preamble of Indian Constitution by the 42nd Amendment were ....
(a) secular
(b) socialist
(c) socialist and secular
(d) democratic and republic

12. What is the minimum age for holding office in the Lok Sabha?
(a) 18 years (b) 30 years
(c) 21 years (d) 25 years

13. At present, how many Fundamental Duties are there in the Indian Constitution?
(a) Twelve (b) Eleven
(c) Ten (d) Nine

14. What type of citizenship is/are provided by the Indian Constitution?
(a) Single Citizenship
(b) Dual Citizenship
(c) Both Single and Dual Citizenship
(d) None of the above

15. According to Constitution of India, which of the following is an Executive body?
(a) Parliament (b) Supreme Court
(c) Ministries (d) Legislative Assembly

16. Which of the following statements is correct about the Fundamental Rights?
(a) Fundamental Rights are known as the cornerstone of Indian Constitution.
(b) Right to Property is a Fundamental Right.
(c) Fundamental Rights are only for citizens.
(d) None of the above

17. Which of the following is not a part of Legislature?
(a) House of People
(b) Council of States
(c) Legislative Assembly
(d) Prime Minister

18. Which of the following is not considered as the pillars of democracy?
(a) Legislature (b) Executive
(c) Judiciary (d) Bureaucracy

19. As per the Constitution of India, Speaker presided over ....
(a) Lok Sabha
(b) Rajya Sabha
(c) Both Lok Sabha and Rajya Sabha
(d) None of the above

20. 'Republic' is a state where ....
(a) the head of the state is an elected person
(b) the head of state is a monarch
(c) there is no head of state
(d) people chose the members of Legislature

21. The word 'Secular' in the Preamble implies that ....
(a) India does not have a state religion or official religion.
(b) India is a religious state.
(c) people of a particular religion can reside in India.
(d) None of the above

22. Identify the person whose statue is shown in the given picture. He was the first Home Minister of Indian Republic.

(a) Dr BR Ambedkar
(b) Dr Rajendra Prasad
(c) Jawaharlal Nehru
(d) Sardar Vallabhbhai Patel

MCQs 2 Marks Questions

23. Match the following.

List I (Leaders)	List II (Role in the making of the Indian Constitution)
A. BR Ambedkar	1. First Vice- President of India
B. GV Mavalankar	2. President of the Constituent Assembly
C. S Radhakrishnan	3. First Speaker of Lok Sabha
D. Rajendra Prasad	4. Vice-President of Chairman of the Drafting Committee

Codes

	A	B	C	D
(a)	4	3	2	1
(b)	4	3	1	2
(c)	3	4	1	2
(d)	1	2	3	4

24. The following words are enshrined in the Preamble to the Constitution of India.

I. Sovereign II. Socialistic
III. Democratic IV. Secular
V. Republic

Which one of the following is the correct order in which they appear in the Preamble?

(a) V, I, II, IV, III
(b) III, II, I, IV, V
(c) III, I, II, V, IV
(d) I, II, IV, III, V

25. Consider the following statements and choose the correct option.

I. In India, the person below 21 years of age cannot vote.
II. In India, all religions are equally respected.

Codes

(a) Only I (b) Only II
(c) Both I and II (d) None of these

26. Match the following.

List I (Year)	List II (Political Event)
A. 1946	1. Constituent Assembly was formed
B. 1950	2. India became independent
C. 1947	3. India became sovereign, democratic and republic
D. 1952	4. The first general election was held

Codes

	A	B	C	D		A	B	C	D
(a)	1	3	2	4	(b)	2	3	4	1
(c)	1	2	3	4	(d)	4	3	2	1

27. Which of the following statements are correct?

I. President is the head of Union Executive.

II. Lok Sabha is the upper house of the Parliament.

III. All Indian citizens are equal in the eyes of the law.

Codes

(a) I and II (b) II and III

(c) I and III (d) I, II and III

28. Consider the following statements and choose the correct option.

I. Fundamental Duties were present in the original Constitution.

II. Amendment of Constitution refers to adding, deleting or bringing changes in the Constitution.

Codes

(a) Only I

(b) Only II

(c) Both I and II

(d) Neither I nor II

29. Read the given statements and identifies which ones are true (T) and which ones are false (F).

I. The Constitution of India is the supreme law of India.

II. Our Constitution is the largest as well as the longest in the world.

III. Madam Bhikaji Cama is the mother of Indian Constitution.

Codes

	I	II	III		I	II	III
(a)	F	T	T	(b)	T	T	T
(c)	F	F	F	(d)	T	F	T

30. According to Indian Constitution, which statement(s) are correct?

I. Union Territories are administered by the Central Government.

II. Parliament make laws for the states.

III. The term 'state' includes the government and Parliament of India.

Codes

(a) I and II (b) II and III

(c) I, II and III (d) I and III

Darken your choice with HB Pencil

1.	ⓐ ⓑ ⓒ ⓓ	6.	ⓐ ⓑ ⓒ ⓓ	11.	ⓐ ⓑ ⓒ ⓓ	16.	ⓐ ⓑ ⓒ ⓓ	21.	ⓐ ⓑ ⓒ ⓓ	26.	ⓐ ⓑ ⓒ ⓓ
2.	ⓐ ⓑ ⓒ ⓓ	7.	ⓐ ⓑ ⓒ ⓓ	12.	ⓐ ⓑ ⓒ ⓓ	17.	ⓐ ⓑ ⓒ ⓓ	22.	ⓐ ⓑ ⓒ ⓓ	27.	ⓐ ⓑ ⓒ ⓓ
3.	ⓐ ⓑ ⓒ ⓓ	8.	ⓐ ⓑ ⓒ ⓓ	13.	ⓐ ⓑ ⓒ ⓓ	18.	ⓐ ⓑ ⓒ ⓓ	23.	ⓐ ⓑ ⓒ ⓓ	28.	ⓐ ⓑ ⓒ ⓓ
4.	ⓐ ⓑ ⓒ ⓓ	9.	ⓐ ⓑ ⓒ ⓓ	14.	ⓐ ⓑ ⓒ ⓓ	19.	ⓐ ⓑ ⓒ ⓓ	24.	ⓐ ⓑ ⓒ ⓓ	29.	ⓐ ⓑ ⓒ ⓓ
5.	ⓐ ⓑ ⓒ ⓓ	10.	ⓐ ⓑ ⓒ ⓓ	15.	ⓐ ⓑ ⓒ ⓓ	20.	ⓐ ⓑ ⓒ ⓓ	25.	ⓐ ⓑ ⓒ ⓓ	30.	ⓐ ⓑ ⓒ ⓓ

Chapter 12

Indian Federalism and Governance

MCQs 1 Mark Questions

1. What is the minimum age to become a President of India?
(a) 50 years (b) 45 years
(c) 25 years (d) 35 years

2. Who is the head of the Union Council of Ministers ?
(a) President (b) Prime Minister
(c) Chief Justice (d) Defence Secretary

3. Prime Minister is appointed by the … .
(a) Council of Ministers
(b) President
(c) Chief Justice of India
(d) Vice-President

4. How many seats are there in Rajya Sabha?
(a) 250 (b) 245 (c) 230 (d) 238

5. How many members of the Rajya Sabha are nominated by the President of India?
(a) 10 (b) 11 (c) 12 (d) 13

6. Which of the following is/are permanent body?
(a) Lok Sabha (b) Rajya Sabha
(c) Both (a) and (b) (d) None of these

7. Members of which of the following houses is/are directly elected by the people?
(a) Rajya Sabha (b) Lok Sabha
(c) Both (a) and (b) (d) None of these

8. Who among the following administers oath to the Prime Minister of India?
(a) Chief Justice of India
(b) President
(c) A Judge of Supreme Court
(d) Speaker

9. Chief Justice of India is appointed by the ………… .
(a) President
(b) Vice-President
(c) Prime Minister
(d) Speaker of Lok Sabha

10. At present, the total number of judges in the Supreme Court including the Chief Justice of Supreme Court is ……… .
(a) 11 (b) 21
(c) 24 (d) 34

11. Who among the following is the Executive head of the state?
(a) President (b) Chief Minister
(c) Governor (d) Prime Minister

12. Which among the following is the lower house of the State Legislature?
(a) Rajya Sabha (b) Lok Sabha
(c) Vidhan Sabha (d) Vidhan Parishad

13. Identify the correctly matched pair.
(a) State Government – State List
(b) Central Government – Union List
(c) Local Government – Residuary power
(d) Central and State Government – Concurrent List

14. What is the tenure of the members of Rajya Sabha?
(a) 5 years (b) 6 years
(c) 4 years (d) 2 years

15. Which of the following is not a unit of local self-governance?
(a) Municipality
(b) Village Panchayat
(c) Municipal Corporation
(d) Lok Adalat

16. Who among the following is the Chairman of NITI Ayog?
(a) President (b) Prime Minister
(c) Governor (d) Home Minister

17. Identify the personality shown in the given picture, who was the first ever woman speaker of Lok Sabha.

(a) Renuka Singh (b) Meira Kumar
(c) Smriti Irani (d) Uma Bharti

18. Complete the given analogy.
Lok Sabha : Speaker :: Rajya Sabha : ?
(a) President
(b) Vice-President
(c) Chairman
(d) Vice-Chairman

19. Who among the following presents budget in the Parliament?
(a) Prime Minister (b) Finance Minister
(c) Finance Secretary (d) Home Minister

MCQs 2 Marks Questions

20. Consider the following statements regarding President and choose the correct option.
I. President can grant pardon to the convicted person.
II. President is the supreme commander of all the three armed forces.

Codes
(a) Only I (b) Only II
(c) Both I and II (d) None of these

21. Chandigarh is located in the North Western part of India. Chandigarh is/are the ……… .
I. Union Territory
II. State
III. State Capital

Codes
(a) I and II (b) I and III
(c) II and III (d) All of these

22. Match the following.

List I (Organisation)	List II (Nature)
A. Supreme Court	1. Legislature
B. Parliament	2. Executive
C. Council of Ministers	3. Judiciary
D. IAS	4. Bureaucracy

Codes

	A	B	C	D		A	B	C	D
(a)	1	2	3	4	(b)	3	1	2	4
(c)	1	3	2	4	(d)	3	2	4	1

23. Which of the following statements is/are correct?

I. The term Panchayati Raj in India signifies rural self-government.

II. In India, there are usually four sessions of Parliament in a year.

III. Lok Sabha has a tenure of 5 years.

Codes

(a) I and II

(b) I and III

(c) II and III

(d) I, II and III

24. Read the given statements and identifies which ones are true (T) and which ones are false (F).

I. The Vice-President of India is an ex-officio chairman of Rajya Sabha.

II. Rajya Sabha is a permanent body as it cannot be dissolved.

III. Lok Sabha is the first chamber of the Parliament and represents the people of India as a whole.

Codes

	I	II	III		I	II	III
(a)	F	T	T	(b)	F	F	F
(c)	T	T	T	(d)	T	F	T

25. Consider the following statements and choose the correct option.

I. Budget is the annual statement of expenditure and income of government.

II. It is passed by the Parliament in the month of April.

Codes

(a) Only I

(b) Only II

(c) Both I and II

(d) None of the above

26. There are two statements marked as Assertion (A) and Reason (R). Mark your answer as per the codes given below.

Assertion (A) President is the first citizen of India and a symbol of unity and integrity.

Reason (R) A bill become an act only after the signature of the President.

Codes

(a) Both A and R are true and R is the correct explanation of A

(b) Both A and R are true, but R is not the correct explanation of A

(c) A is true, but R is false

(d) A is false, but R is true

27. Arrange the courts with the highest power being in the top and court with the lowest power in the bottom.

I. High Court

II. Supreme Court

III. Taluka Court

IV. District Court

Codes

(a) III, I, IV, II

(b) II, I, IV, III

(c) II, IV, I, III

(d) I, II, IV, III

Darken your choice with HB Pencil

1. ⓐ ⓑ ⓒ ⓓ	6. ⓐ ⓑ ⓒ ⓓ	11. ⓐ ⓑ ⓒ ⓓ	16. ⓐ ⓑ ⓒ ⓓ	21. ⓐ ⓑ ⓒ ⓓ	26. ⓐ ⓑ ⓒ ⓓ
2. ⓐ ⓑ ⓒ ⓓ	7. ⓐ ⓑ ⓒ ⓓ	12. ⓐ ⓑ ⓒ ⓓ	17. ⓐ ⓑ ⓒ ⓓ	22. ⓐ ⓑ ⓒ ⓓ	27. ⓐ ⓑ ⓒ ⓓ
3. ⓐ ⓑ ⓒ ⓓ	8. ⓐ ⓑ ⓒ ⓓ	13. ⓐ ⓑ ⓒ ⓓ	18. ⓐ ⓑ ⓒ ⓓ	23. ⓐ ⓑ ⓒ ⓓ	
4. ⓐ ⓑ ⓒ ⓓ	9. ⓐ ⓑ ⓒ ⓓ	14. ⓐ ⓑ ⓒ ⓓ	19. ⓐ ⓑ ⓒ ⓓ	24. ⓐ ⓑ ⓒ ⓓ	
5. ⓐ ⓑ ⓒ ⓓ	10. ⓐ ⓑ ⓒ ⓓ	15. ⓐ ⓑ ⓒ ⓓ	20. ⓐ ⓑ ⓒ ⓓ	25. ⓐ ⓑ ⓒ ⓓ	

Chapter 13

Political Parties and Elections

MCQs 1 Mark Questions

1. Which of the following countries is an example of a two-party system?
   (a) United States of America
   (b) Russia
   (c) China
   (d) Canada

2. What proportion of seats are reserved in rural and urban local bodies for women candidates?
   (a) One-third of the total seats
   (b) Two-third of the total seats
   (c) Half of the total seats
   (d) One-fourth of the total seats

3. Which among the following states has the largest number of Lok Sabha seats?
   (a) West Bengal (b) Gujarat
   (c) Assam (d) Rajasthan

4. In India, political parties are recognised by ………………. .
   (a) Election Commission of India
   (b) The Finance Commission
   (c) State Election Commission
   (d) None of the above

5. When was coalition government formed for the first time in India ?
   (a) 1967 (b) 1977
   (c) 1987 (d) 1997

6. The clock is the symbol of which Indian political party?
   (a) National Congress Party
   (b) Communist Party of India
   (c) Bahujan Samaj Party
   (d) Rashtriya Janata Dal

7. Who appoints the Chief Election Commissioner of India?
   (a) The Chief Justice of India
   (b) The Prime Minister of India
   (c) The President of India
   (d) The Speaker of the Lok Sabha

8. The Chief Election Commissioner of India holds office for a period of ………………. .
   (a) six years
   (b) during the pleasure of the President
   (c) for six years or till the age of 65 years, whichever is earlier.
   (d) for five years or till the age of 60 years, whichever is earlier

9. Which one of the following is considered as the best form of government?
(a) Democracy (b) Dictatorship
(c) Monarchy (d) Military rule

10. Name the authority which conduct Panchayat election in India.
(a) Election Commission of India
(b) State Election Commission
(c) Panchayati Raj Department
(d) Gram Sabha

11. Elections in India for Parliament and State Legislatures are conducted by ....
(a) President
(b) State Election Commission
(c) Governor
(d) Election Commission of India

12. Which party is only allowed to rule in China?
(a) Socialist party (b) Communist party
(c) Liberal party (d) Maoist party

13. The party whose election symbol shown in the given picture, is founded in which year?

(a) 1910 (b) 1980
(c) 1990 (d) 2000

14. Complete the given analogy.
BJP : Lotus :: ? : Broom
(a) Bahujan Samaj Party
(b) Nationalist Congress Party
(c) Aam Aadmi Party
(d) Janata Dal United

15. Which among the following is not a national party in India?
(a) Aam Aadmi Party
(b) Bharatiya Janata Party
(c) Congress Party
(d) Rashtriya Janata Dal

16. What is the correct meaning of the term general election?
(a) State election
(b) Elections in the district
(c) Speaker's election
(d) Election in all constituencies

17. Who among the following was the first Chief Election Commissioner of India?
(a) TN Seshan
(b) VS Ramadevi
(c) Sukumar Sen
(d) Kalyan Sundaram

18. The machine in the picture is used for conducting election. When was this machine is used in India for the first time?

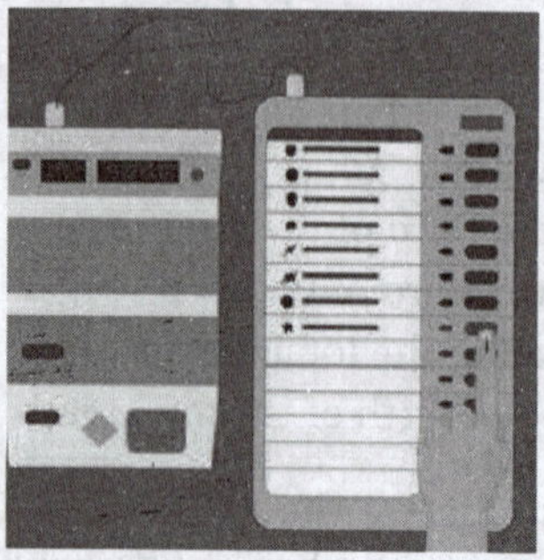

(a)1982 (b) 1989
(c) 1992 (d) 2002

19. The election to the Lok Sabha is based on the principle of ....
(a) Universal Adult Franchise
(b) Proportional Representation
(c) Referandum
(d) Plebiscite

MCQs 2 Marks Questions

20. Election Commission of India conducts election for

I. Lok Sabha
II. Rajya Sabha
III. State Legislative Assembly

Codes

(a) Only I
(b) Both I and II
(c) I, II and III
(d) Both II and III

21. The Proportional Representative System by means of the single transferable vote is followed in the election of which of the following?

I. Vice-President
II. Members of Legislative Assembly
III. Members of Legislative Council

Codes

(a) I and III
(b) I and II
(c) II and III
(d) All of the above

22. There are two statements marked as Assertion (A) and Reason (R). Mark your answer as per the codes given below.

Assertion (A) India adopted a multi-party system.

Reason (R) India has more than 750 parties registered with Election Commission.

Codes

(a) Both A and R are true and R is the correct explanation of A
(b) Both A and R are true, but R is not the correct explanation of A
(c) A is true, but R is false
(d) A is false, but R is true

23. Read the given statements and identifies which ones are true (T) and which ones are false (F).

I. Uttar Pradesh has the largest number of Lok Sabha seats.
II. The minimum age for voting in India is 18 years.
III. The slogan of Garibi Hatao was given in Lok Sabha election in 1971.

Codes

	I	II	III
(a)	F	T	T
(b)	F	F	F
(c)	T	T	T
(d)	T	F	T

24. Which of the following parties do not included in the National Democratic Alliance?

I. Janata Dal United
II. Lok Janshakti Party
III. Trinamool Congress

Codes

(a) I and II
(b) I and III
(c) II and III
(d) Only I

Darken your choice with HB Pencil

1.	ⓐ ⓑ ⓒ ⓓ	5.	ⓐ ⓑ ⓒ ⓓ	9.	ⓐ ⓑ ⓒ ⓓ	13.	ⓐ ⓑ ⓒ ⓓ	17.	ⓐ ⓑ ⓒ ⓓ	21.	ⓐ ⓑ ⓒ ⓓ
2.	ⓐ ⓑ ⓒ ⓓ	6.	ⓐ ⓑ ⓒ ⓓ	10.	ⓐ ⓑ ⓒ ⓓ	14.	ⓐ ⓑ ⓒ ⓓ	18.	ⓐ ⓑ ⓒ ⓓ	22.	ⓐ ⓑ ⓒ ⓓ
3.	ⓐ ⓑ ⓒ ⓓ	7.	ⓐ ⓑ ⓒ ⓓ	11.	ⓐ ⓑ ⓒ ⓓ	15.	ⓐ ⓑ ⓒ ⓓ	19.	ⓐ ⓑ ⓒ ⓓ	23.	ⓐ ⓑ ⓒ ⓓ
4.	ⓐ ⓑ ⓒ ⓓ	8.	ⓐ ⓑ ⓒ ⓓ	12.	ⓐ ⓑ ⓒ ⓓ	16.	ⓐ ⓑ ⓒ ⓓ	20.	ⓐ ⓑ ⓒ ⓓ	24.	ⓐ ⓑ ⓒ ⓓ

Chapter 14

International Organisation

MCQs 1 Mark Questions

1. Who was the first General Secretary of UNO?
(a) Dag Hammarskjold
(b) U Thant
(c) Trygve Lie
(d) Kurt Waldheim

2. The United Nations Conference on Trade and Development (UNCTAD) is located at which of the following places?
(a) Geneva (b) Rome
(c) Paris (d) Vienna

3. The headquarters of the UNESCO is located in ....
(a) Rome (b) Geneva
(c) New York (d) Paris

4. The headquarters of Food and Agriculture Organisation is located in which of the following cities?
(a) Washington (b) Paris
(c) Madrid (d) Rome

5. Choose the country which is not a member of SAARC.
(a) Nepal (b) Bangladesh
(c) Afghanistan (d) Myanmar

6. Who was the first Indian to be President of UN General Assembly?
(a) Vijay Lakshmi Pandit
(b) Ramesh Bhandari
(c) Natwar Singh
(d) Krishna Menon

7. Which of the following is the headquarters of World Trade Organisation (WTO)?
(a) New York (b) Geneva
(c) Madrid (d) Paris

8. Which of the following is a cultural organisation?
(a) UNESCO (b) ILO
(c) WHO (d) FAO

9. The International Court of Justice is located at ....
(a) Geneva (b) Hague
(c) Amsterdam (d) Vienna

10. The working language(s) of the UNESCO is/are ....
(a) French
(b) English
(c) English and French
(d) English, French and Russian

11. What is the meaning of INTERPOL?
(a) International Political Conference
(b) International Criminal Police Organisation
(c) International Association of Police Officers
(d) None of the above

12. Complete the given analogy.
NAFTA : America : : SAFTA : ?
(a) Asia (b) Europe (c) Africa (d) Oceania

13. New Development Bank (BRICS Development Bank) is headquartered in which of the following countries?
(a) Japan (b) South Africa
(c) Brazil (d) China

14. Complete the given analogy.
WHO : Health : : WTO : ?
(a) Solar Energy
(b) Law of Sea
(c) Intellectual Property Rights
(d) World Trade

15. The emblem given in the picture is the emblem of which organisation?

(a) UNO (b) WTO
(c) IMF (d) SAARC

16. Identify the headquarter of United Nations Educational Scientific and Cultural Organisation (UNESCO).
(a) Paris (b) Geneva
(c) Madrid (d) New York

17. Name the animal which is used as the logo of the World Wide Fund for Nature (WWF).
(a) Deer (b) Panda
(c) Lion (d) Elephant

18. Where is the permanent secretariat of the SAARC?
(a) New Delhi (b) Islamabad
(c) Colombo (d) Kathmandu

19. Who was the first Indian to make a speech in Hindi before the UN General Assembly?
(a) Moraji Desai
(b) Atal Bihari Vajpayee
(c) Lal Bahadur Shastri
(d) Lal Krishna Advani

20. When did United Nations Environment Programme establish?
(a) 1962 (b) 1972
(c) 1965 (d) 1960

21. Identify the correctly matched pair(s).

	Institution		Established in
(a)	World Health Organisation	–	1948
(b)	International Labour Organisation	–	1919
(c)	United Nations International Children's Emergency Fund	–	1946
(d)	All of the above		

22. How many institutions come under United Nations Organisation?
(a) 6 (b) 3
(c) 4 (d) 5

23. .... is the headquarter of United Nations Economic and Social Council.
(a) Paris (b) New York
(c) Rome (d) Vienna

MCQs 2 Marks Questions

24. Which of the following statements is/are not correct with reference to the World Trade Organisation (WTO)?

I. The objective of the WTO is to ensure optimal use of the world's resources by establishing a rule-based trading system.

II. WTO was established in 1985.

Codes

(a) Only I (b) Only II
(c) Both I and II (d) Neither I nor II

25. There are two statements marked as Assertion (A) and Reason (R). Mark your answer as per the codes given below.

Assertion (A) International Solar Alliance was founded in 2018.

Reason (R) India is one of the founding members of International Solar Alliance.

Codes

(a) Both A and R are true and R is the correct explanation of A
(b) Both A and R are true, but R is not the correct explanation of A
(c) A is true, but R is false
(d) A is false, but R is true

26. Consider the following statements regarding ASEAN and choose the correct option.

I. ASEAN was established on 8th August, 1967 in Bangkok.

II. The body is headquartered in Manila, Philippines.

Codes

(a) Only I (b) Only II
(c) Both I and II (d) None of these

27. Identify the international organisation with the help of the information given below.

- This organisation is the powerful grouping of the world's leading emerging market economies, namely India, China, Brazil, Russia and South Africa.
- It was founded in June, 2009. Its mechanism aims to promote peace, security, development and cooperation.

(a) WTO (b) BRICS
(c) UNCTAD (d) SAARC

28. Read the given statements and identifies which ones are true (T) and which ones are false (F).

I. The headquarters of World Food Programme is in Rome.

II. South Africa is a part of BRICS.

III. Klaus Schwab is the founder of World Economic Forum.

Codes

	I	II	III		I	II	III
(a)	F	T	T	(b)	F	F	F
(c)	T	T	T	(d)	T	T	F

29. Which of the following statements are incorrect about SAARC?

I. SAARC is a group of South Asian Nation.

II. SAARC is headquartered at New Delhi.

III. Iran is a member country of SAARC.

Codes

(a) I and II (b) II and III
(c) I and III (d) All of these

Darken your choice with HB Pencil

1.	ⓐ ⓑ ⓒ ⓓ	6.	ⓐ ⓑ ⓒ ⓓ	11.	ⓐ ⓑ ⓒ ⓓ	16.	ⓐ ⓑ ⓒ ⓓ	21.	ⓐ ⓑ ⓒ ⓓ	26.	ⓐ ⓑ ⓒ ⓓ
2.	ⓐ ⓑ ⓒ ⓓ	7.	ⓐ ⓑ ⓒ ⓓ	12.	ⓐ ⓑ ⓒ ⓓ	17.	ⓐ ⓑ ⓒ ⓓ	22.	ⓐ ⓑ ⓒ ⓓ	27.	ⓐ ⓑ ⓒ ⓓ
3.	ⓐ ⓑ ⓒ ⓓ	8.	ⓐ ⓑ ⓒ ⓓ	13.	ⓐ ⓑ ⓒ ⓓ	18.	ⓐ ⓑ ⓒ ⓓ	23.	ⓐ ⓑ ⓒ ⓓ	28.	ⓐ ⓑ ⓒ ⓓ
4.	ⓐ ⓑ ⓒ ⓓ	9.	ⓐ ⓑ ⓒ ⓓ	14.	ⓐ ⓑ ⓒ ⓓ	19.	ⓐ ⓑ ⓒ ⓓ	24.	ⓐ ⓑ ⓒ ⓓ	29.	ⓐ ⓑ ⓒ ⓓ
5.	ⓐ ⓑ ⓒ ⓓ	10.	ⓐ ⓑ ⓒ ⓓ	15.	ⓐ ⓑ ⓒ ⓓ	20.	ⓐ ⓑ ⓒ ⓓ	25.	ⓐ ⓑ ⓒ ⓓ		

Chapter 15

General Awareness

(Books & Authors, Awards & Honours, Capital & Currencies, Research Institute, Place of the World)

MCQs 1 Mark Questions

1. Who among the following wrote the book 'India Wins Freedom'?
(a) Akhilesh Tilotia
(b) Amitav Ghosh
(c) Abdul Kalam Azad
(d) AB Vajpayee

2. Name the author of the book 'Anandamath'.
(a) Rabindranath Tagore
(b) Mahatma Gandhi
(c) Bankim Chandra Chatterjee
(d) BR Ambedkar

3. Identify the personality who wrote the book 'An Autobiography'.
(a) Sardar Patel
(b) Jawaharlal Nehru
(c) Atal Bihari Vajpayee
(d) S Radhakrishnan

4. Which of the following is the highest Gallantry Award in India?
(a) Param Vishishta Seva Medal
(b) Param Vir Chakra
(c) Kirti Chakra
(d) Vir Chakra

5. The first Indian to receive Noble Prize in Literature was ....
(a) Mother Teresa
(b) CV Raman
(c) Rabindranath Tagore
(d) Sarojini Naidu

6. The only Indian to win the Nobel Prize in Physics is ....
(a) Dr JC Bose
(b) Dr CV Raman
(c) Dr Vikram Sarabhai
(d) Dr HJ Bhabha

7. Who among the following was the first recipient of Rajiv Gandhi's Khel Ratna Award?
(a) Viswanathan Anand
(b) Leander Peas
(c) Kapil Dev
(d) Limba Ram

8. Pulitzer Prize is awarded for outstanding work in the field of ....
(a) Science and Technology
(b) Environmental Studies
(c) Literature and Journalism
(d) International Understanding

9. Marie Curie was awarded with the Nobel Prize twice in the fields of ....
(a) Physics and Medicine
(b) Chemistry and Peace
(c) Physics and Chemistry
(d) Chemistry and Medicine

10. What is the currency of Israel?
(a) Togrog (b) Rial
(c) Israeli Dinar (d) New Shekel

11. Complete the given analogy.
China : Yuan :: Japan : ?
(a) Dollar (b) Pound
(c) Yen (d) Euro

12. Which of the following is the capital of Canada?
(a) Ottowa (b) Hanoi
(c) Canbara (d) Moxico

13. Vienna is the national capital and largest city of ....
(a) Austria (b) Russia
(c) Spain (d) Syria

14. Complete the given analogy.
Sri Lanka : Colombo :: Bhutan : ?
(a) Thimpu (b) Jakarta
(c) Manila (d) Madrid

15. Identify the incorrectly matched pair.

Countries		Currency
(a) Saudi Arabia	–	Riyal
(b) Indonesia	–	Dong
(c) Iran	–	Rial
(d) Iraq	–	Dinar

16. The headquarters of Indian Space Research Institute is located in which city?
(a) Shimla
(b) Chennai
(c) Bengaluru
(d) Chandigarh

17. The Indian Council of Agricultural Research has its headquarters at ....
(a) Aurangabad (b) New Delhi
(c) Samastipur (d) Bengaluru

18. Indian Institute of Remote Sensing is located at which city?
(a) Dehradun (b) Shimla
(c) Kullu (d) Bilaspur

19. The International Community of Red Cross is headquartered at ....
(a) Geneva (b) Rome
(c) Paris (d) London

20. The headquarters of Defence Research and Development Organisation is situated at ....
(a) Bengaluru (b) Pune
(c) New Delhi (d) Hyderabad

21. Suez Canal is located in which of the following countries?
(a) Turkey (b) Egypt
(c) Iran (d) Iraq

22. Which of the following countries is called the 'Island of Pearls' ?
(a) Thailand (b) Bahrain
(c) Japan (d) Switzerland

23. Identify the statue shown in the given picture which is one of the seven wonders of the world situated in Italy.

(a) Leaning Tower of Pisa
(b) Statue of Liberty
(c) Colosseum
(d) Pyramids of Giza

24. The building in the picture is considered as the highest building in the world. Where is this building located?

(a) London (b) Dubai
(c) Riyadh (d) New York

25. Kalahari Desert is located at ....
(a) South Africa (b) North Africa
(c) South America (d) West Asia

MCQs 2 Marks Questions

26. Which of the following books have been written by Abu'l Fazl?
I. Ain-i-Akbari II. Akbar-Nama
III. Tuzuk-i-Akbari

Codes
(a) I and II (b) I and III
(c) I, II and III (d) None of these

27. There are two statements marked as Assertion (A) and Reason (R). Mark your answer as per the codes given below.

Assertion (A) The Port of Shanghai is the world's busiest port.

Reason (R) Shanghai is the commercial centre of China and the country's most cosmopolitan city.

Codes
(a) Both A and R are true, and R is the correct explanation of A
(b) Both A and R are true, but R is not the correct explanation of A
(c) A is true, but R is false
(d) A is false, but R is true

28. Identify the personality with the help of the information given below.
- He was the writer of Geeta Rahashya.
- He started two newspapers Kesari and Maratha during Indian freedom struggle.

(a) Mahatma Gandhi
(b) Bal Gangadhar Tilak
(c) Aurobindo Ghosh
(d) Lala Lajpat Rai

29. Which of the following statements are incorrect?
I. Padma Vibhushan is the highest Civilian Award in India.
II. Ashoka Chakra is India' highest Peacetime Military Award.
III. Arjuna Award is given in the field of sports.
IV. Dronacharya Award is given to primary school teachers.

Codes
(a) I, II and III
(b) I, II and IV
(c) I and IV
(d) II and IV

30. Match the following.

List I (Countries)	List II (Capital)
A. Japan	1. Rome
B. China	2. Tokyo
C. Italy	3. Berlin
D. Germany	4. Beijing

Codes

	A	B	C	D
(a)	2	4	1	3
(b)	1	2	3	4
(c)	4	2	3	1
(d)	3	2	1	4

31. Consider the following statements and choose the correct option.

I. World famous Disneyland is located in America.

II. London is situated on the bank of river Thames.

III. Kaaba, a holy place for Muslim is located at Mecca.

Codes

(a) I and III (b) I and II

(c) II and III (d) All of these

32. Consider the following statements and choose the incorrect option.

I. Pisa is a town in France which is famous for one of the seven wonders of world.

II. Stockholm is the capital city of Sweden.

III. Rhur is a city in Italy which is famous for coal field.

Codes

(a) I and III (b) Only II

(c) Only III (d) II and III

33. Match the following.

List I (Books)	**List II** (Author)
A. Kadambari	1. Banabhatta
B. Godan	2. Kalidasa
C. Meghdoot	3. Premchand
D. Panchatantra	4. Vishnu Sharma

Codes

	A	B	C	D
(a)	2	4	1	3
(b)	1	3	2	4
(c)	4	2	3	1
(d)	3	2	1	4

34. Which of the following countries are located in South Asia?

I. Maldives

II. Mexico

III. Nepal

IV. Barmuda

Codes

(a) I and II

(b) I and III

(c) II and IV

(d) I, II and IV

35. Nobel Prize is awarded in which of the following fields?

I. Physics

II. Chemistry

III. Geography

IV. Economics

Codes

(a) I, II and IV

(b) I and III

(c) I and II

(d) All of the above

Darken your choice with HB Pencil

1. ⓐ ⓑ ⓒ ⓓ	7. ⓐ ⓑ ⓒ ⓓ	13. ⓐ ⓑ ⓒ ⓓ	19. ⓐ ⓑ ⓒ ⓓ	25. ⓐ ⓑ ⓒ ⓓ	31. ⓐ ⓑ ⓒ ⓓ
2. ⓐ ⓑ ⓒ ⓓ	8. ⓐ ⓑ ⓒ ⓓ	14. ⓐ ⓑ ⓒ ⓓ	20. ⓐ ⓑ ⓒ ⓓ	26. ⓐ ⓑ ⓒ ⓓ	32. ⓐ ⓑ ⓒ ⓓ
3. ⓐ ⓑ ⓒ ⓓ	9. ⓐ ⓑ ⓒ ⓓ	15. ⓐ ⓑ ⓒ ⓓ	21. ⓐ ⓑ ⓒ ⓓ	27. ⓐ ⓑ ⓒ ⓓ	33. ⓐ ⓑ ⓒ ⓓ
4. ⓐ ⓑ ⓒ ⓓ	10. ⓐ ⓑ ⓒ ⓓ	16. ⓐ ⓑ ⓒ ⓓ	22. ⓐ ⓑ ⓒ ⓓ	28. ⓐ ⓑ ⓒ ⓓ	34. ⓐ ⓑ ⓒ ⓓ
5. ⓐ ⓑ ⓒ ⓓ	11. ⓐ ⓑ ⓒ ⓓ	17. ⓐ ⓑ ⓒ ⓓ	23. ⓐ ⓑ ⓒ ⓓ	29. ⓐ ⓑ ⓒ ⓓ	35. ⓐ ⓑ ⓒ ⓓ
6. ⓐ ⓑ ⓒ ⓓ	12. ⓐ ⓑ ⓒ ⓓ	18. ⓐ ⓑ ⓒ ⓓ	24. ⓐ ⓑ ⓒ ⓓ	30. ⓐ ⓑ ⓒ ⓓ	

Chapter 16

Media and Entertainment

MCQs 1 Mark Questions

1. Which one of the following is print media?
   (a) Newspaper
   (b) Telephone
   (c) Radio
   (d) Television

2. Which type of media offer a large variety of information to suit the taste of different readers?
   (a) Electronic Media
   (b) Print Media
   (c) Mass Media
   (d) All of the above

3. Identify which among the following is the main source of income of media.
   (a) Advertisements
   (b) Articles
   (c) General news
   (d) None of the above

4. Which word is used to refer a TV or radio programme that is widely transmitted?
   (a) Publish (b) Broadcast
   (c) Censorship (d) Public protest

5. Which country has the largest newspaper circulation in the world?
   (a) China (b) India
   (c) USA (d) None of these

6. Select the country which produce the maximum number of films.
   (a) India (b) Germany
   (c) USA (d) Nigeria

7. TRAI stands for ....
   (a) Training Rural Achievement in India
   (b) Telecom Regulatory Authority of India
   (c) Television Regulation Advertising in India
   (d) Teaching Radio Act in India

8. Which among the following is a multimedia software?
   (a) Window media player
   (b) Microsoft word
   (c) Adobe audition
   (d) Adobe page maker

9. Complete the given analogy.
   Print Media : Magazine : : Electronic Media : ?
   (a) Newspaper (b) Whatsapp
   (c) Radio News Channel (d) Magazine

10. Which of the following denotes internet radio broadcast?
(a) Broadcast
(b) Narrowcast
(c) Podcast
(d) Telecast

11. Identify the type of media which is shown in the given picture.

(a) Print Media
(b) Electronic Media
(c) Social Media
(d) None of the above

12. Which of the following was the first newspaper published in India?
(a) Bengal Gazette (b) Times of India
(c) Hindustan Times (d) Pioneer

13. Film and Television Institute of India is located at ....
(a) Pune (b) Mumbai
(c) Delhi (d) Kolkata

14. Which among the following was the first movie of India?
(a) Alam Ara
(b) Kisan Kanya
(c) Raja Harishchandra
(d) Mughal-e-Azam

15. Which was the first Indian movie to win an Oscar?
(a) Slumdog Millionaire
(b) Mother India
(c) Gandhi
(d) None of the above

16. Identify the incorrectly matched pair.

Media	**Related to**
(a) Internet	– Website
(b) Support Media	– Advertisement
(c) Print Media	– E-mail
(d) Broadcast Media	– Television

17. Which among the following is the highest film award in entertainment?
(a) Prem Nazir Award
(b) Dada Saheb Phalke Award
(c) Raja Harischandra Award
(d) Satyajit Ray Award

18. Name the educational channel of Doordarshan.
(a) Bharti (b) Vidyabharti
(c) ETV (d) Gyandarshan

19. Who was considered as the inventor of television?
(a) Thomas Alva Edison
(b) Charles Babbage
(c) John Logie Baird
(d) Marconi

MCQs 2 Marks Questions

20. Which among the following are parts of media?
I. Radio II. Digital marketing
III. Visual effects IV. Print
Codes
(a) I, II and IV (b) I and IV
(c) I and II (d) All of these

21. There are two statements marked as Assertion (A) and Reason (R). Mark your answer as per the codes given below.
Assertion (A) Press Council of India was established in 1992.
Reason (R) It is a self regulating body to regulate Print Media.

Codes

(a) Both A and R are true and R is the correct explanation of A
(b) Both A and R are true, but R is not the correct explanation of A
(c) A is true, but R is false
(d) A is false, but R is true

22. Which of the following is/are not the part of entertainment industry?

I. Film II. Magazine III. Sports Code

Codes

(a) I and II (b) I and III
(c) II and III (d) Only III

23. Match the following.

List I (Media)	**List II** (Founder)
A. Instagram	1. Sergey Brin and Larry Page
B. Facebook	2. Kevin Systrom
C. Goggle	3. Mark Zuckerberg
D. Gmail	4. Paul Buchheit

Codes

	A	B	C	D		A	B	C	D
(a)	1	2	3	4	(b)	4	3	2	1
(c)	1	4	3	2	(d)	2	3	1	4

24. Read the given statements and identifies which ones are true (T) and which ones are false (F).

I. Udant Martand is the first Hindi newspaper of India.
II. India's first talkie film was Alam Ara.
III. Dada Saheb Phalke is known as the Father of Indian Cinema.

Codes

	I	II	III
(a)	T	F	T
(b)	F	F	T
(c)	T	T	T
(d)	F	F	F

25. Which of the following statements is/are incorrect?

I. Newspaper became the first mass medium of circulating information.
II. E-mail is the most common means of written communication.

Codes

(a) Only I
(b) Only II
(c) I and II
(d) None of the above

Darken your choice with HB Pencil

1. ⓐ ⓑ ⓒ ⓓ	6. ⓐ ⓑ ⓒ ⓓ	11. ⓐ ⓑ ⓒ ⓓ	16. ⓐ ⓑ ⓒ ⓓ	21. ⓐ ⓑ ⓒ ⓓ
2. ⓐ ⓑ ⓒ ⓓ	7. ⓐ ⓑ ⓒ ⓓ	12. ⓐ ⓑ ⓒ ⓓ	17. ⓐ ⓑ ⓒ ⓓ	22. ⓐ ⓑ ⓒ ⓓ
3. ⓐ ⓑ ⓒ ⓓ	8. ⓐ ⓑ ⓒ ⓓ	13. ⓐ ⓑ ⓒ ⓓ	18. ⓐ ⓑ ⓒ ⓓ	23. ⓐ ⓑ ⓒ ⓓ
4. ⓐ ⓑ ⓒ ⓓ	9. ⓐ ⓑ ⓒ ⓓ	14. ⓐ ⓑ ⓒ ⓓ	19. ⓐ ⓑ ⓒ ⓓ	24. ⓐ ⓑ ⓒ ⓓ
5. ⓐ ⓑ ⓒ ⓓ	10. ⓐ ⓑ ⓒ ⓓ	15. ⓐ ⓑ ⓒ ⓓ	20. ⓐ ⓑ ⓒ ⓓ	25. ⓐ ⓑ ⓒ ⓓ

Chapter 17

Science and Technology

MCQs 1 Mark Questions

1. Who among the following gave the first evidence of the Big Bang Theory?
(a) Edwin Hubble (b) Albert Einstein
(c) S Chandrasekhar (d) Stephen Hawking

2. Anatomy deals with the study of ....
(a) functions of human body
(b) human nature
(c) structure of human body
(d) functions of human body parts

3. Who among the following discovered the atom bomb?
(a) Otto Hahn (b) Albert Einstein
(c) Edison (d) Lord Rutherford

4. The unit of energy produced by food in the human body is called ....
(a) watt (b) DNA
(c) calorie (d) ampere

5. Who is regarded as the pioneer of atomic energy in India?
(a) APJ Abdul Kalam
(b) Homi J Bhabha
(c) Raja Ramanna
(d) Homi Sethna

6. The theory of relativity was putforth by which of the following scientists?
(a) Albert Einstein (b) Edison
(c) Galileo (d) Newton

7. Radio-activity was first discovered by ....
(a) Pasteur (b) Newton
(c) Watson (d) Madam Curie

8. Who was the first man who placed his foot on the Moon?
(a) Leonov (b) Neil Armstrong
(c) Michael Collins (d) James Van Allen

9. The term cytology is the study related to ....
(a) plant (b) bone
(c) cells (d) environment

10. Complete the given analogy.
Osteology : Bones : : Pathology : ?
(a) Disease (b) Virus
(c) Blood (d) Medicine

11. Plants receive their nutrients mainly from ....
(a) chlorophyll (b) atmosphere
(c) light (d) soil

12. Complete the given analogy.

Dengue : Virus : : Malaria : ?

(a) Protozoa (b) Bacteria
(c) Fungus (d) None of these

13. Most commonly used material in making bulletproof jackets is ....

(a) formalin (b) coal-tar
(c) kevlar (d) fullerene

14. Plants that grow in saline water are called......... .

(a) Halophytes (b) Hydrophytes
(c) Mesophytes (d) Thallophytes

15. Who was awarded the Noble Prize for the discovery of Neutrons?

(a) James Chadwick (b) JJ Thomson
(c) Rutherford (d) Niels Bohr

16. What was the name of the space shuttle that landed man on the Moon?

(a) Apollo (b) Challenger
(c) Columbia (d) Eagle

17. Who is known as the Father of the Indian Space Programme?

(a) CV Raman
(b) APJ Kalam
(c) Satish Dhawan
(d) Vikram Sarabhai

18. Where is Bhabha Atomic Research Centre (BARC) situated?

(a) Bombay
(b) New Delhi
(c) Chennai
(d) Bengaluru

19. Which among the following is responsible for Itai-Itai disease?

(a) Cadmium
(b) Lead
(c) Nickel
(d) Mercury

20. Goitre and the enlarged thyroid gland are mainly diagnosed in patients with deficiencies of which of the following minerals?

(a) Iron (b) Iodine
(c) Calcium (d) Phosphorus

21. Identify the device as shown in the picture given below.

(a) Fighter aircraft
(b) Communication satellite
(c) Nuclear reactor
(d) Experimental satellite

22. India's first heavy water plant was established at which place?

(a) Maharashtra
(b) Punjab
(c) Uttar Pradesh
(d) Madhya Pradesh

MCQs 2 Marks Questions

23. Which of the followings are satellites launched by ISRO?

I. Mangalyaan –II
II. Gaganyaan
III. Chandrayaan–II
IV. Sputnik

Codes

(a) I and II
(b) I and III
(c) I, II and III
(d) None of the above

24. Match the following.

List I (Scientists)	List II (Inventions)
A. Newton	1. Gravity
B. Edison	2. Radio
C. Marconi	3. Electric Bulb
D. Wright Brothers	4. Aeroplane

Codes

	A	B	C	D		A	B	C	D
(a)	1	3	2	4	(b)	2	3	4	1
(c)	1	2	3	4	(d)	2	4	3	1

25. Which of the following vitamins is /are water soluble?

I. Vitamin C II. Vitamin B
III. Vitamin D

Codes

(a) Only I (b) Only II
(c) I and II (d) I, II and III

26. Consider the following statements and choose the correct option.

I. Mitochondria is the energy house of cell.
II. Cell is the basic unit of life.
III. Tissues are made up of cell.

Codes

(a) I and II (b) I and III
(c) I, II and III (d) None of these

27. Which of the following are not a part of white spectrum?

I. Voilet II. Margenta
III. Orange IV. Green

Codes

(a) I, II and III
(b) I, II and IV
(c) I, III and IV
(d) All of the above

28. Identify the following with the help of the information given below.

- It was launched by the Indian Space Research Organisation (ISRO) and was India's first mission to the Moon.
- The spacecraft was launched on 22nd October, 2008 by a modified version of the PSLV C-11 from Satish Dhawan Space Centre, Sriharikota, Andhra Pradesh.

(a) Sputnik
(b) Apollo
(c) Chandrayaan
(d) Rohini

29. Read the given statements and identifies which ones are true (T) and which ones are false (F).

I. The Deficiency of Vitamin E leads to weakness in muscles.
II. Vitamin A deficiency is the main cause of blindness in children worldwide.
III. Vitamin C helps in blood clotting.

Codes

	I	II	III
(a)	T	T	T
(b)	F	T	T
(c)	T	T	F
(d)	F	F	T

Darken your choice with HB Pencil

1.	ⓐ ⓑ ⓒ ⓓ	6.	ⓐ ⓑ ⓒ ⓓ	11.	ⓐ ⓑ ⓒ ⓓ	16.	ⓐ ⓑ ⓒ ⓓ	21.	ⓐ ⓑ ⓒ ⓓ	26.	ⓐ ⓑ ⓒ ⓓ
2.	ⓐ ⓑ ⓒ ⓓ	7.	ⓐ ⓑ ⓒ ⓓ	12.	ⓐ ⓑ ⓒ ⓓ	17.	ⓐ ⓑ ⓒ ⓓ	22.	ⓐ ⓑ ⓒ ⓓ	27.	ⓐ ⓑ ⓒ ⓓ
3.	ⓐ ⓑ ⓒ ⓓ	8.	ⓐ ⓑ ⓒ ⓓ	13.	ⓐ ⓑ ⓒ ⓓ	18.	ⓐ ⓑ ⓒ ⓓ	23.	ⓐ ⓑ ⓒ ⓓ	28.	ⓐ ⓑ ⓒ ⓓ
4.	ⓐ ⓑ ⓒ ⓓ	9.	ⓐ ⓑ ⓒ ⓓ	14.	ⓐ ⓑ ⓒ ⓓ	19.	ⓐ ⓑ ⓒ ⓓ	24.	ⓐ ⓑ ⓒ ⓓ	29.	ⓐ ⓑ ⓒ ⓓ
5.	ⓐ ⓑ ⓒ ⓓ	10.	ⓐ ⓑ ⓒ ⓓ	15.	ⓐ ⓑ ⓒ ⓓ	20.	ⓐ ⓑ ⓒ ⓓ	25.	ⓐ ⓑ ⓒ ⓓ		

Chapter 18

Computer

MCQs 1 Mark Questions

1. Which one of the following is not an Operating System (OS)?
(a) Windows 10
(b) Linux
(c) DOS
(d) MS Excel

2. In the virtual world, WWW stands for ....
(a) World Without Windows
(b) World Wide Web
(c) World Wide Web Applications
(d) World Wide Warehouse

3. Which one of the following is different from other members?
(a) Google (b) Windows
(c) Linux (d) Mac

4. Which of the following is not an input device?
(a) Mouse
(b) Light pen
(c) Keyboard
(d) VDU

5. The software that allows user to surf the internet is called ....
(a) multimedia application
(b) browser
(c) Internet Service Provider (ISP)
(d) search engine

6. Complete the given analogy.
Firefox : ? : : Trojan : Virus
(a) Web browser
(b) Driver
(c) Operating system
(d) Programme language

7. Which of the following is an example of non-volatile memory?
(a) Cache memory
(b) RAM
(c) ROM
(d) None of the above

8. Which web browser was developed by Google?
(a) Internet Explorer
(b) Firefox
(c) Safari
(d) Chrome

9. Identify the device shown in the given picture which is used to connect with the internet network.

(a) Router (b) Wifi
(c) Network (d) None of these

10. Which of the following refers to a small, single-site network?
(a) LAN (b) WAN
(c) ROM (d) RAM

11. What is the number of 'function-key' in the keyboard?
(a) 105 (b) 9
(c) 12 (d) 6

12. Which among the following is the largest software company in India?
(a) Infosys (b) WIPRO
(c) TCS (d) HCL

13. What is the full form of USB?
(a) Ubit Stall Bit
(b) Universal Serial Bus
(c) Unit Serial Bus
(d) Universal Stall Bus

14. First page of website is termed as ....
(a) 1st page
(b) home page
(c) desktop
(d) All of the above

15. Identify the name of first electronic computer.
(a) Param (b) ENIAC
(c) EENIAC (d) INTERNET

16. Virtual keyboards protect the computer against ....
(a) password theft
(b) trojan programs
(c) spyware
(d) All of the above

17. Which is/are not a type of secondary memory?
(a) Cache Memory
(b) Hard Disk
(c) Random Access Memory (RAM)
(d) All of the above

MCQs 2 Marks Questions

18. There are two statements marked as Assertion (A) and Reason (R). Mark your answer as per the codes given below.

Assertion (A) PARAM is the first Super Computer of India .

Reason (A) PARAM stands for 'PARAllel machine' and was developed by the Centre for Development of Advanced Computing (CDAC).

Codes
(a) Both A and R are true and R is the correct explanation of A
(b) Both A and R are true, but R is not the correct explanation of A
(c) A is true, but R is false
(d) A is false, but R is true

19. Match the following.

List I (Generation)	List II (Technology used)
A. First Generation	1. Microprocessor
B. Second Generation	2. Vacuum Tubes
C. Third Generation	3. Integrated Circuit
D. Fourth Generation	4. Transistor

Codes

	A	B	C	D		A	B	C	D
(a)	2	4	3	1	(b)	1	3	2	4
(c)	3	2	1	4	(d)	1	2	3	4

20. Which of the following languages does the computer understand?
I. Computer understand only C language.
II. Computer understand only Binary language.

Codes
(a) Only I (b) Only II
(c) Both I and II (d) None of these

21. Which of the following computer languages is/are written in Binary codes only?

I. Pascal

II. Machine language

III. C language

Codes

(a) Only I (b) Only II

(c) Only III (d) I, II and III

22. Identify the type of computer with the help of the information given below.

- This computer reads data using measurement and some program scale.
- It calculates by measuring continuous changes in the physical quantities.

(a) Analog Computer

(b) Hybrid Computer

(c) Digital Computer

(d) None of the above

23. Which of the following are not a type of computer on the basis of operation?

I. Digital II. Analog

III. Hybrid

Codes

(a) I and II (b) I and III

(c) I, II and III (d) None of these

24. Consider the following statements and choose the correct option.

I. The process of transferring files from your computer to internet is called uploading.

II. IP address is given to a computer through which it is connected to the network.

Codes

(a) Only I (b) Only II

(c) I and II (d) None of these

Darken your choice with HB Pencil

1.	ⓐ ⓑ ⓒ ⓓ	5.	ⓐ ⓑ ⓒ ⓓ	9.	ⓐ ⓑ ⓒ ⓓ	13.	ⓐ ⓑ ⓒ ⓓ	17.	ⓐ ⓑ ⓒ ⓓ	21.	ⓐ ⓑ ⓒ ⓓ
2.	ⓐ ⓑ ⓒ ⓓ	6.	ⓐ ⓑ ⓒ ⓓ	10.	ⓐ ⓑ ⓒ ⓓ	14.	ⓐ ⓑ ⓒ ⓓ	18.	ⓐ ⓑ ⓒ ⓓ	22.	ⓐ ⓑ ⓒ ⓓ
3.	ⓐ ⓑ ⓒ ⓓ	7.	ⓐ ⓑ ⓒ ⓓ	11.	ⓐ ⓑ ⓒ ⓓ	15.	ⓐ ⓑ ⓒ ⓓ	19.	ⓐ ⓑ ⓒ ⓓ	23.	ⓐ ⓑ ⓒ ⓓ
4.	ⓐ ⓑ ⓒ ⓓ	8.	ⓐ ⓑ ⓒ ⓓ	12.	ⓐ ⓑ ⓒ ⓓ	16.	ⓐ ⓑ ⓒ ⓓ	20.	ⓐ ⓑ ⓒ ⓓ	24.	ⓐ ⓑ ⓒ ⓓ

Chapter 19

Sport

MCQs 1 Mark Questions

1. Mithali Raj is a famous player of which sport?
(a) Football (b) Cricket
(c) Chess (d) Hockey

2. Who among the following won the first Olympic medal individually for independent India?
(a) KD Jadhav
(b) Milkha Singh
(c) Harishchandra Birajdar
(d) Dhyan Chand

3. Mirabai Chanu is associated with which sport?
(a) Tennis (b) Cricket
(c) Weightlifting (d) Gymnastics

4. Grand Slam is used in which of the following games?
(a) Lawn Tennis (b) Football
(c) Badminton (d) None of these

5. Who is the first Indian woman to win an Olympic Silver Medal?
(a) Saina Nehwal
(b) PV Sindhu
(c) Rituparna Das
(d) Tanvi Lad

6. In which year, the first Asian Games was held?
(a) 1951 (b) 1952
(c) 1953 (d) 1954

7. FIFA is the global regulatory body of which sport?
(a) Hockey (b) Football
(c) Cricket (d) Tennis

8. Who was the first Indian woman to get an Olympic Medal?
(a) PT Usha (b) Sania Mirza
(c) Aarti Shah (d) Karnam Malleswari

9. What is the full form of IPL?
(a) Indian Premier League
(b) Indo-Pakistan League
(c) International Premier League
(d) Indian Players League

10. Olympic Medalists of India Bajrang Punia and Ravi Dhaiya associated with which sport?
(a) Boxing (b) Shooting
(c) Wrestling (d) Judo

11. Thomas Cup and Uber Cup are prestigious trophies of ....
(a) badminton (b) lawn tennis
(c) table tennis (d) golf

12. Complete the given analogy.
Cricket : Umpire :: Football : ?
(a) Refree (b) Line Umpire
(c) Scorer (d) None of these

13. The athelete with the Prime Minister shown in the image is regarded as the queen of Indian track. She was awarded with Padma Shri Award. Identify the athelete.

(a) PT Usha (b) Hima Das
(c) Dutee Chand (d) None of these

14. Dyer test is associated with ....
(a) tennis (b) badminton
(c) athletics (d) football

15. Federation Cup in India is associated with which game/ sport?
(a) Hockey (b) Football
(c) Basketball (d) Badminton

16. The Asian Games are organised after every ....
(a) 3 year (b) 4 year
(c) 5 year (d) 6 year

17. Which country is known as the father of cricket?
(a) India (b) England
(c) Sri Lanka (d) None of these

18. Identify the incorrectly matched pair.

	Sportsperson		Sports
(a)	MS Dhoni	–	Cricket
(b)	Bhaichung Bhutia	–	Football
(c)	Chetan Anand	–	Badminton
(d)	Geeta Phogat	–	Shooting

19. Name the country which have won the first T20 World Cup.
(a) Sri Lanka (b) Pakistan
(c) India (d) England

20. Jawaharlal Nehru stadium is in ....
(a) Chennai (b) New Delhi
(c) Kolkata (d) Mumbai

21. Where was the first Olympic Games held?
(a) Canada (b) England
(c) Australia (d) Jamaica

MCQs 2 Marks Questions

22. Match the following.

List I (Player)	List II (Game)
A. Rahul Dravid	1. Football
B. Dhyan Chand	2. Cricket
C. David Beckham	3. Hockey
D. Mary Kom	4. Boxing

Codes

	A	B	C	D		A	B	C	D
(a)	2	3	1	4	(b)	1	3	2	4
(c)	2	3	4	1	(d)	1	2	3	4

23. Which of the following games are not included in Olympic Games?
I. Cricket II. Polo
III. Hockey
Codes
(a) I and II (b) I and III
(c) II and III (d) All of these

24. There are two statements marked as Assertion (A) and Reason (R). Mark your answer as per the codes given below.
Assertion (A) India's highest sporting honour is Khel Ratna Award.
Reason (R) The first recipient of this award was Chess Grandmaster Viswanathan Anand.

Codes

(a) Both A and R are true and R is the correct explanation of A

(b) Both A and R are true, but R is not the correct explanation of A

(c) A is true, but R is false

(d) A is false, but R is true

25. Which of the following statements is/are correct?

I. Dronacharya Award is related to sports.

II. Durand Cup Tournament is related to football.

Codes

(a) Only I (b) Only II

(c) Both I and II (d) None of these

26. Consider the following statements and choose the incorrect option.

I. Butterfly stroke is associated with swimming.

II. Manu Bhaker is the famous player of badminton.

III. Grandmaster is the word related to tennis.

Codes

(a) I and III (b) I and II

(c) II and III (d) I, II and III

27. Which of the following statements is/are correct?

I. Sachin Tendulkar was the first cricketer who awarded Rajiv Gandhi Khel Ratna Award.

II. The word checkmate is used in the sport of Kabaddi.

Codes

(a) Only I (b) Only II

(c) Both I and II (d) None of these

28. Match the following.

List I (Games)		List II (Related term)
A. Cricket	1.	Penalty
B. Hockey	2.	Googly
C. Football	3.	Double fault
D. Badminton	4.	Foul

Codes

	A	B	C	D
(a)	1	3	2	4
(b)	2	1	4	3
(c)	3	2	1	4
(d)	1	2	3	4

29. Read the given statements and identifies which ones are true (T) and which ones are false (F).

I. The first Asian Games were held in New Delhi.

II. Davis Cup is associated with lawn tennis.

III. There are 5 players in each side of basketball games.

Codes

	I	II	III		I	II	III
(a)	T	F	T	(b)	T	T	T
(c)	F	T	F	(d)	F	F	T

Darken your choice with HB Pencil

1. ⓐ ⓑ ⓒ ⓓ	6. ⓐ ⓑ ⓒ ⓓ	11. ⓐ ⓑ ⓒ ⓓ	16. ⓐ ⓑ ⓒ ⓓ	21. ⓐ ⓑ ⓒ ⓓ	26. ⓐ ⓑ ⓒ ⓓ
2. ⓐ ⓑ ⓒ ⓓ	7. ⓐ ⓑ ⓒ ⓓ	12. ⓐ ⓑ ⓒ ⓓ	17. ⓐ ⓑ ⓒ ⓓ	22. ⓐ ⓑ ⓒ ⓓ	27. ⓐ ⓑ ⓒ ⓓ
3. ⓐ ⓑ ⓒ ⓓ	8. ⓐ ⓑ ⓒ ⓓ	13. ⓐ ⓑ ⓒ ⓓ	18. ⓐ ⓑ ⓒ ⓓ	23. ⓐ ⓑ ⓒ ⓓ	28. ⓐ ⓑ ⓒ ⓓ
4. ⓐ ⓑ ⓒ ⓓ	9. ⓐ ⓑ ⓒ ⓓ	14. ⓐ ⓑ ⓒ ⓓ	19. ⓐ ⓑ ⓒ ⓓ	24. ⓐ ⓑ ⓒ ⓓ	29. ⓐ ⓑ ⓒ ⓓ
5. ⓐ ⓑ ⓒ ⓓ	10. ⓐ ⓑ ⓒ ⓓ	15. ⓐ ⓑ ⓒ ⓓ	20. ⓐ ⓑ ⓒ ⓓ	25. ⓐ ⓑ ⓒ ⓓ	

Practice Set 01

Time : 60 Mins. Max. Marks : 60

General Instructions

1. This question paper contains 50 questions.
2. All questions are compulsory. There is no negative marking.
3. Q. No. 1 to 40 are of 1 mark each and Q. No. 41 to 50 are of 2 marks each.
4. Use HB pencil / Blue ball point pen to mark your choice of answer by darkening the circles on the OMR Sheet.

MCQs 1 Mark Questions

1. Who was the first Governor-General of the independent India?
(a) Sardar Patel
(b) Jawaharlal Nehru
(c) C Rajagopalachari
(d) Lord Mountbatten

2. The Governor of a state is appointed by the President on the advice of the ………… .
(a) Prime Minister
(b) Vice- President
(c) Chief Minister
(d) Chief Justice

3. Name the person who wrote the book 'Hind Swaraj'.
(a) Jawaharlal Nehru
(b) Mahatma Gandhi
(c) MG Ranade
(d) Bal Gangadhar Tilak

4. Which one of the following awards is presented for the outstanding achievements in the music industry?
(a) Nobel Prize
(b) Grammy Award
(c) Man Booker Prize
(d) Bharat Ratna

5. Name the woman who was the first women judge of Delhi High Court.
(a) Sujata Manohar
(b) Rama Paul
(c) Leila Seth
(d) Anna Chandy

6. Who among the following is/are not directly appointed by the people of India?
(a) Vice-President
(b) President
(c) Member of Lok Sabha
(d) Both (a) and (b)

7. Complete the given analogy :
Harshcharita : Banabhatta : :
Meghadootam : ?
(a) Kalidasa (b) Al- Idrisi
(c) Pulakeshin (d) Harisena

8. Who was the first woman President of India?
(a) Sheila Dikshit
(b) Pratibha Patil
(c) Vasundhra Raje
(d) Najma Heptulla

9. …………… is the currency of the country China.
(a) Pound (b) Dinnar
(c) Renminbi (d) Euro

10. Which of the following awards is not related with the field of sports?
(a) Arjuna Award
(b) Dronacharya Award
(c) Dhyanchand Award
(d) Norman Borlaug Award

11. Select the correct chronology of Indian mountain ranges from North to South.
(a) Karakoram, Himadri, Shivalik, Zaskar
(b) Karakoram, Shivalik, Himadri, Zaskar
(c) Zaskar, Shivalik, Himadri, Karakoram
(d) Karakoram, Zaskar, Himadri, Shivalik

12. Which among the following is the world's deepest lake in the world?
(a) Baikal Lake (b) Caspian Lake
(c) Victoria Lake (d) Titicaca Lake

13. Complete the given analogy.
Arunachal Pradesh : Itanagar : : Mizoram : ?
(a) Imphal (b) Shillong
(c) Kohima (d) Aizawl

14. Ustad Zakir Hussain is associated with which of the following instruments?
(a) Sarod (b) Sitar (c) Tabla (d) Shehnai

15. Name the oldest mountain range in India.
(a) Aravalli (b) Satpura
(c) Nilgiri (d) Himalayas

16. How much time was taken by the Constituent Assembly to complete the draft of our Constitution?
(a) 2 years, 10 months, 20 days
(b) 2 years, 9 months, 20 days
(c) 2 years, 11 months ,18 days
(d) 2 years, 10 months ,5 days

17. Forests that remain green throughout the year are called ....
(a) Deciduous Forests (b) Alpine Forests
(c) Evergreen Forests (d) Monsoon Forests

18. Golden Quadrilateral Project for the Development of National Highways was initiated by ....
(a) P V Narasimha Rao
(b) IK Gujral
(c) Manmohan Singh
(d) Atal Bihari Vajpayee

19. Identify the incorrectly matched pair.

Railway Zone	Headquarters
(a) North-Eastern Railway	Gorakhpur
(b) South-Eastern Railway	Bhubaneswar
(c) Eastern-Railway	Kolkata
(d) South-East Central Railway	Bilaspur

20. Which of the following places is famous for chikankari work, which is a traditional art of embroidery?
(a) Lucknow (b) Hyderabad
(c) Jaipur (d) Mysore

21. Complete the given analogy.
Nearest planet : Mercury : : Farthest planet : ?
(a) Saturn (b) Venus
(c) Uranus (d) Neptune

22. International Monetary Fund or IMF began operations in which of the following years?
(a) 1945 (b) 1947
(c) 1951 (d) 1963

23. Identify the name of the famous personality who compose the Allahabad Pillar Inscription.
(a) Dandin (b) Harisena
(c) Sudraka (d) Banabhatta

24. Complete the given analogy.
Africa : Congo River : : ? : Rio Grande River
(a) Australia (b) North America
(c) Asia (d) South America

25. Which sportsperson is famous by the name 'Haryana Hurricane'?
(a) Kapil Dev
(b) Saina Nehwal
(c) Vijendra Singh
(d) Mansoor Ali Khan Pataudi

26. The World Food Programme (WFP) is the food assistance branch of the United Nations. Where is it's headquarter?
(a) Paris (b) Brussels
(c) Rome (d) New York

27. Which among the following is the highest literacy award given by the Government of India?
(a) Kalidas Samman
(b) Jnanpith Award
(c) Sahitya Akademi Award
(d) Saraswati Samman

28. Name the personality who have written the book named 'Exam Warrior'.
(a) Rajnath Singh (b) Sushma Swaraj
(c) Smriti Irani (d) Narendra Modi

29. The book 'Poverty and Un-British Rule in India' is written by ....
(a) Mahatma Gandhi
(b) Jawaharlal Nehru
(c) Dadabhai Naoroji
(d) Indira Gandhi

30. Which of the following is the memory in CPU that holds programme instructions, input data and the output information produced?
(a) System
(b) Secondary Memory
(c) Primary Memory
(d) None of the above

31. Name the first communication satellite which was launched in 1962.
(a) Intelset (b) Early Bird
(c) Insat (d) Intersputnik

32. Identify the medium of communication as shown in the picture given below.

(a) Telephone (b) Fax machine
(c) Electronic Mail (d) Cordless Phone

33. Which of the following mountains has the largest peaks in the world?
(a) Aravali Mountain
(b) Karakoram Range
(c) Mount Everest
(d) Mount Everest

34. The Gonds tribes is found in which of the following states of India?
(a) Assam
(b) Madhya Pradesh
(c) Jammu and Kashmir
(d) Haryana

35. Name the components of air that are harmful to living organism.
(a) Oxygen and carbon dioxide
(b) Dust and smoke
(c) Smoke and water vapour
(d) Nitrogen and oxygen

36. Which of the following is the deepest landlocked protected port of India?
(a) Haldia
(b) Jawaharlal Nehru
(c) Chennai
(d) Visakhapatnam

37. Who was the first woman in India to climb Mount Everest?
(a) Premlata Agarwal
(b) Bachendri Pal
(c) Santosh Yadav
(d) Arunima Sinha

38. Athens is the capital of which South-Eastern European country?
(a) Greece (b) Germany
(c) Finland (d) Czech Republic

39. Which type of vegetation is found only in the North-Western part of India?
(a) Mangrove Forests
(b) Thorn Forests and Scrubs
(c) Tropical Deciduous Forests
(d) Tropical Evergreen Forests

40. The 'Chhatrapati Shivaji International Airport' is located at which of the following cities?
(a) Lucknow (b) Pune
(c) Mumbai (d) Nagpur

MCQs 2 Marks Questions

41. Consider the following statements and choose the correct option.
I. Western Railway Zone is the largest railway zone of the Indian railways with respect to length of railway tracks in kilometers.
II. Metro railway with its headquarters at Kolkata is the latest addition to railway zones of India.
Codes
(a) Only I
(b) Only II
(c) Both I and II
(d) Neither I nor II

42. Read the following statements about Mother Teresa and choose the correct option.
I. She was the first and only Indian to receive Nobel Peace Prize.
II. She was awarded with Bharat Ratna in 1980.
Codes
(a) Only I
(b) Only II
(c) Both I and II
(d) Neither I nor II

43. Match the following.

	List I (Features)	List II (Borrowed from)
A.	Preamble	1. Ireland
B.	Parliamentary form of Government	2. USSR
C.	Fundamental Duties	3. Britain
D.	Directive Principles of State Policy	4. USA

Codes

	A	B	C	D
(a)	4	3	2	1
(b)	3	4	1	2
(c)	2	3	4	1
(d)	1	2	3	4

44. There are two statements marked as Assertion (A) and Reason (R). Mark your answer as per the codes given below.
Assertion (A) The Governor is appointed by the President of our country.
Reason (R) The President is the head of state of the Republic of India.
Codes
(a) Both A and R are true and R is the correct explanation of A
(b) Both A and R are true, but R is not the correct explanation of A
(c) A is true, but R is false
(d) A is false, but R is true

45. Match the following.

List I (Heritage Sites of India)	List II (Location)
A. Kedarnath Temple	1. Punjab
B. Sanchi Stupa	2. Uttarakhand
C. Golden Temple	3. Gujarat
D. Somnath Temple	4. Madhya Pradesh

Codes

	A	B	C	D
(a)	4	3	2	1
(b)	2	3	1	4
(c)	2	4	1	3
(d)	3	4	2	1

46. Read the given statements and identifies which ones are true (T) and which ones are false (F).

I. The headquarters of United Nations Organisation is located at New York.

II. International Monetary Fund or IMF began operations in the year 1947.

III. World Trade Organisation issues the rules of global trades.

Codes

	I	II	III
(a)	T	T	T
(b)	F	T	T
(c)	T	T	F
(d)	F	F	T

47. Identify the mountain ranges of India marked as A and B marked on the map given below.

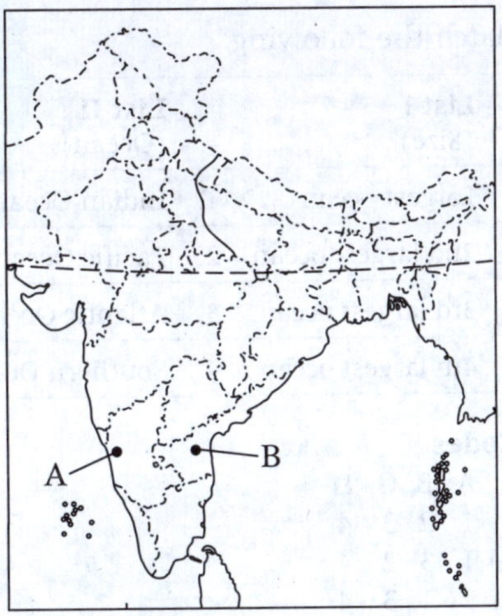

Codes

	A	B
(a)	Nilgiris	Middle Himalayas
(b)	Satpura	Western Ghats
(c)	Deccan Plateau	Satpura
(d)	Western Ghats	Eastern Ghats

48. Identify the place of India with the help of the information given below.

- It is a sacred place of the Sikhs in Amritsar. It is known as the Golden Temple.
- Operation Blue Star was held in this pilgrimage spot.
- It has been nominated as an UNESCO World Heritage Site.

(a) Sri Akal Takht Sahib
(b) Damdama Sahib
(c) Anandpur Sahib
(d) Harmandir Sahib

49. Match the following.

List I (Size)	**List II** (Ocean)
A. Largest ocean	1. Indian Ocean
B. 2nd largest ocean	2. Pacific Ocean
C. 3rd largest ocean	3. Atlantic Ocean
D. 4th largest ocean	4. Southern Ocean

Codes

	A	B	C	D
(a)	1	2	3	4
(b)	1	3	2	4
(c)	2	1	3	4
(d)	2	3	1	4

50. Read the given statements and identifies which ones are true (T) and which ones are false (F).

I. National Police Academy is located at Hyderabad.

II. Central Drug Research Institute is located at Lucknow (UP).

III. The headquarters of World Bank is in Washington DC.

Codes

	I	II	III
(a)	T	T	T
(b)	F	T	T
(c)	T	T	F
(d)	F	F	T

Darken your choice with HB Pencil

1.	ⓐ ⓑ ⓒ ⓓ	10.	ⓐ ⓑ ⓒ ⓓ	19.	ⓐ ⓑ ⓒ ⓓ	28.	ⓐ ⓑ ⓒ ⓓ	37.	ⓐ ⓑ ⓒ ⓓ	46.	ⓐ ⓑ ⓒ ⓓ
2.	ⓐ ⓑ ⓒ ⓓ	11.	ⓐ ⓑ ⓒ ⓓ	20.	ⓐ ⓑ ⓒ ⓓ	29.	ⓐ ⓑ ⓒ ⓓ	38.	ⓐ ⓑ ⓒ ⓓ	47.	ⓐ ⓑ ⓒ ⓓ
3.	ⓐ ⓑ ⓒ ⓓ	12.	ⓐ ⓑ ⓒ ⓓ	21.	ⓐ ⓑ ⓒ ⓓ	30.	ⓐ ⓑ ⓒ ⓓ	39.	ⓐ ⓑ ⓒ ⓓ	48.	ⓐ ⓑ ⓒ ⓓ
4.	ⓐ ⓑ ⓒ ⓓ	13.	ⓐ ⓑ ⓒ ⓓ	22.	ⓐ ⓑ ⓒ ⓓ	31.	ⓐ ⓑ ⓒ ⓓ	40.	ⓐ ⓑ ⓒ ⓓ	49.	ⓐ ⓑ ⓒ ⓓ
5.	ⓐ ⓑ ⓒ ⓓ	14.	ⓐ ⓑ ⓒ ⓓ	23.	ⓐ ⓑ ⓒ ⓓ	32.	ⓐ ⓑ ⓒ ⓓ	41.	ⓐ ⓑ ⓒ ⓓ	50.	ⓐ ⓑ ⓒ ⓓ
6.	ⓐ ⓑ ⓒ ⓓ	15.	ⓐ ⓑ ⓒ ⓓ	24.	ⓐ ⓑ ⓒ ⓓ	33.	ⓐ ⓑ ⓒ ⓓ	42.	ⓐ ⓑ ⓒ ⓓ		
7.	ⓐ ⓑ ⓒ ⓓ	16.	ⓐ ⓑ ⓒ ⓓ	25.	ⓐ ⓑ ⓒ ⓓ	34.	ⓐ ⓑ ⓒ ⓓ	43.	ⓐ ⓑ ⓒ ⓓ		
8.	ⓐ ⓑ ⓒ ⓓ	17.	ⓐ ⓑ ⓒ ⓓ	26.	ⓐ ⓑ ⓒ ⓓ	35.	ⓐ ⓑ ⓒ ⓓ	44.	ⓐ ⓑ ⓒ ⓓ		
9.	ⓐ ⓑ ⓒ ⓓ	18.	ⓐ ⓑ ⓒ ⓓ	27.	ⓐ ⓑ ⓒ ⓓ	36.	ⓐ ⓑ ⓒ ⓓ	45.	ⓐ ⓑ ⓒ ⓓ		

Practice Set 02

Time : 60 Mins. Max. Marks : 60

General Instructions

1. This question paper contains 50 questions.
2. All questions are compulsory. There is no negative marking.
3. Q. No. 1 to 40 are of 1 mark each and Q. No. 41 to 50 are of 2 marks each.
4. Use HB pencil / Blue ball point pen to mark your choice of answer by darkening the circles on the OMR Sheet.

MCQs 1 Mark Questions

1. Name the country which shares land boundaries with India in the East.
(a) Bhutan (b) Bangladesh
(c) China (d) Vietnam

2. .... Hills of Tamil Nadu lie at the junction of the Eastern and Western Ghats.
(a) Anamudi (b) Nilgiri
(c) Mahendragiri (d) Aravalli

3. Where is the headquarters of South-Central Railway located?
(a) Madhya Pradesh (b) Mumbai
(c) Secunderabad (d) Vijayawada

4. FIFA is the global regulatory body of which sport?
(a) Hockey (b) Football
(c) Cricket (d) Tennis

5. Venus is considered as Earth's-twin because ....
(a) it is a brightest planet in the night sky
(b) it is the hottest planet in the Solar System
(c) its size and shape are similar to that of the Earth
(d) it has no Moons

6. On which date, Indian Constitution was finally signed by the members of the Constituent Assembly?
(a) 26th November, 1949
(b) 24th January, 1950
(c) 26th November, 1950
(d) 24th January, 1949

7. Which of the following is the longest side of the Golden Quadrilateral?
(a) Delhi – Mumbai
(b) Mumbai – Chennai
(c) Chennai – Kolkata
(d) Kolkata – Delhi

8. Identify the correctly matched pair.
(a) Sultanpur Bird Sanctuary – Rajasthan
(b) Kaziranga National Park – Arunachal Pradesh
(c) Bandipur National park – Karnataka
(d) Gir National Park – Madhya Pradesh

9. Which of these layers of the atmosphere consists of the ozone layer that is responsible for absorbing the Ultra-Violet (UV) light?
(a) Troposphere (b) Mesosphere
(c) Stratosphere (d) None of these

10. Which one of the following is the other name of the holy book Adi-Granth?
(a) Adi-Puran
(b) Guru Granth Sahib
(c) Gurumukhi
(d) Kuran

11. Identify the continent which has the highest number of countries.
(a) Asia
(b) Europe
(c) North America
(d) Africa

12. The first meeting of Indian National Congress was held in Bombay in 1885 AD under the leadership of ....
(a) Dadabhai Naoroji
(b) Sir C Sankaran Nair
(c) WC Banerjee
(d) Badruddin Tyabji

13. Who among the following was the chairperson of the Provincial Constitution Committee of the Constituent Assembly?
(a) Jawaharlal Nehru
(b) Sardar Vallabhbhai Patel
(c) Dr BR Ambedkar
(d) JB Kripalani

14. In which year, first general elections to Lok Sabha were held in India?
(a) 1948 (b) 1949
(c) 1950 (d) 1951

15. Name the first Chief Election Commissioner of India.
(a) KVK Sundaram
(b) SP Sen Verma
(c) Sukumar Sen
(d) Rajmannar

16. Which of the following is known as most dense layer of the Earth?
(a) Core (b) Crust
(c) Mantle (d) Magma

17. Name the biggest island located in the Indian Ocean.
(a) Madagascar (b) Greenland
(c) Sumatra (d) Baffin Island

18. In how many zones, Indian railway has been divided?
(a) 14 (b) 16
(c) 18 (d) 20

19. In which of the following festivals, is boat races a special feature?
(a) Pongal (b) Navratri
(c) Rongali Bihu (d) Onam

20. The headquarters of World Intellectual Property Organisation (WIPO) is located in ....
(a) Paris (b) Madrid
(c) New York (d) Geneva

21. What is the name of the first supercomputer developed in India?
(a) Atlas (b) Param
(c) Titan (d) Pratyush

22. The presence of which among the following salts in water causes 'Blue Baby Syndrome'?
(a) Sulphates (b) Chlorides
(c) Carbonates (d) Nitrates

23. Who is the author of the book 'Freedom Behind Bars'?
(a) Kiran Bedi
(b) Jawaharlal Nehru
(c) Nelson Mandela
(d) Sheikh Abdullah

24. Identify the incorrectly matched pair.

	Device		Input/Output
(a)	Scanner	–	Output device
(b)	Printer	–	Output device
(c)	Joystick	–	Input device
(d)	Keyboard	–	Input device

25. Complete the given analogy.

Russia : Ruble :: ? : Kyat

(a) Sri Lanka (b) Myanmar
(c) Bangladesh (d) China

26. Identify the physiographic division of India as shown in the picture given below.

(a) Peninsular plateau
(b) Mountain ranges
(c) Coastal area
(d) Northern plains

27. Where is the headquarters of World Health Organisation located?

(a) New Delhi, India
(b) London, UK
(c) Geneva, Switzerland
(d) None of the above

28. Identify the incorrectly matched pair.

	Personalities		**Instruments Related to**
(a)	Bismillah Khan	–	Shehnai
(b)	Amzad Ali Khan	–	Sarod
(c)	Birju Maharaj	–	Kathak
(d)	Zakir Hussain	–	Harmonium

29. Identify the sportsperson among the following who is first Olympic Gold Medallist.

(a) Neeraj Chopra (b) Abhinav Bindra
(c) Rishabh Pant (d) Sunil Chhetri

30. In which year did India become the champion of world cup cricket for the first time?

(a) 1981 (b) 1982
(c) 1983 (d) 1986

31. Which of the following networking devices forwards data packets between computer networks?

(a) Router (b) Gateway
(c) Switch (d) Hub

32. Satish Dhawan Space Centre is located in which of the following states?

(a) Karnataka (b) Andhra Pradesh
(c) Tamil Nadu (d) Kerala

33. Complete the given analogy.

Narmada River : Arabian Sea :: ? : Bay of Bengal

(a) Tapi River
(b) Krishna River
(c) Sabarmati River
(d) Mahi River

34. Which one of the following is the national sports of USA?

(a) Football (b) Hockey
(c) Table Tennis (d) Baseball

35. 'Madhubani', a style of folk paintings, is popular in which of the following states in India?

(a) Uttar Pradesh (b) Rajasthan
(c) Madhya Pradesh (d) Bihar

36. The famous species of tree 'Sundari' is found in ....

(a) Tropical Deciduous Forests
(b) Tropical Rainforests
(c) Mangrove Forests
(d) Himalaya Mountains

37. Identify the incorrectly matched pair.

	Countries	**Currency**
(a)	Israel	– Rial
(b)	Japan	– Yen
(c)	China	– Dollar
(d)	UK	– Sterling Pound

38. Complete the given analogy.

Cricket : Third man : : Football : ?

(a) Throwin (b) Digpass
(c) Free Style (d) None of these

39. Which country has the lengthiest Constitution in the world?

(a) United States (b) France
(c) India (d) Japan

40. .... was the first Indian woman to be President of the Indian National Congress and to be appointed an Indian state governor.

(a) Indira Gandhi (b) Sarojini Naidu
(c) Annie Besant (d) Sucheta Kriplan

MCQs 2 Marks Questions

41. Which of the following statements with regard to national parks is/are correct?

I. Kaziranga National Park is a protected area. It is located in Assam.
II. Hemis National Park is the largest national park in India, located in Jammu and Kashmir.

Codes

(a) Only I (b) Both I and II
(c) Neither I nor II (d) Only II

42. Match the following.

List I (Tribal Groups)	List II (States)
A. Garo	1. Mizoram
B. Bhutiya	2. Arunachal Pradesh
C. Kuki	3. Uttarakhand
D. Apatani	4. Meghalaya

Codes

	A	B	C	D
(a)	3	1	2	4
(b)	2	1	4	3
(c)	3	1	2	4
(d)	4	3	1	2

43. There are two statements marked as Assertion (A) and Reason (R). Mark your answer as per the codes given below.

Assertion (A) Pratibha Patil is the first woman President of India.

Reason (R) The President is the chief commander of all the three Indian forces.

Codes

(a) Both A and R are true and R is the correct explanation of A
(b) Both A and R are true, but R is not the correct explanation of A
(c) A is true, but R is false
(d) A is false, but R is true

44. Read the given statements and identifies which ones are true (T) and which ones are false (F).

I. Mount Godwin Austen is the second highest mountain peak in the world.
II. River Brahmaputra has its origin in Tibet near Mansarover Lake.
III. Gujarat is the state with the longest coastline.

Codes

	I	II	III		I	II	III
(a)	T	T	T	(b)	F	T	T
(c)	T	T	F	(d)	F	F	T

45. Identify the continent which has been shown in the picture given below.

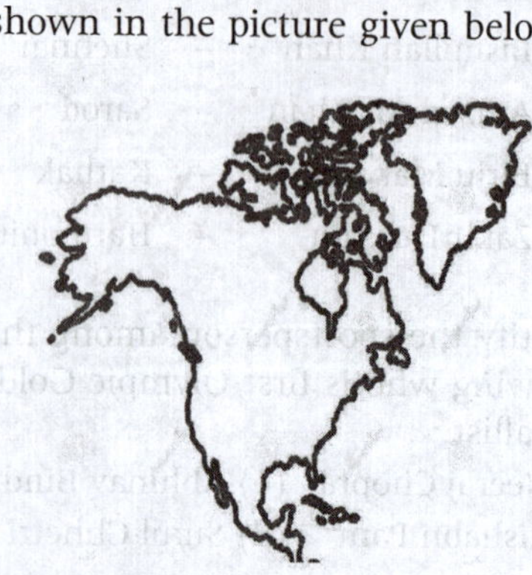

(a) Australia (b) North America
(c) South America (d) Africa

46. Identify the person with the help of the information given below.

- 'He is the the head of the state.
- He supervises the overall functioning of all the political institutions in India, so that they operate in harmony to achieve the objectives of the state.'

(a) President
(b) Speaker of the Lok Sabha
(c) Prime Minister
(d) Vice-President

47. Match the following.

List I (Heritages Sites of India)	List I (Location)
A. Khajuraho Temple	1. Odisha
B. Meenakshi Temple	2. Maharashtra
C. Ellora Cave	3. Tamil Nadu
D. Sun Temple	4. Madhya Pradesh

Codes

	A	B	C	D		A	B	C	D
(a)	4	3	2	1	(b)	1	3	4	2
(c)	2	1	3	4	(d)	3	4	2	1

48. Read the given statements and identifies which ones are true (T) and which ones are false (F).

I. Gulbadan Begum was the author of the book 'Humayun Nama'.
II. APJ Abdul Kalam was the author of the book 'Wings of Fire'.
III. Rabindranath Tagore was the author of the popular book 'Gitanjali'.

Codes

	I	II	III		I	II	III
(a)	T	T	T	(b)	F	T	T
(c)	T	T	F	(d)	F	F	T

49. Which among the following statements is/are correct about the Atlantic Ocean?

I. It is the second largest ocean in the world.
II. It separates the 'Old World' from the 'New World'.
III. It occupies an elongated triangle-shaped basin.

Codes

(a) I and II (b) Only I
(c) I and III (d) I, II, III

50. Match the following.

List I (Country)	List II (Capital)
A. Russia	1. Beijing
B. Australia	2. Moscow
C. China	3. Canberra
D. Egypt	4. Cairo

Codes

	A	B	C	D
(a)	1	3	4	2
(b)	4	3	1	2
(c)	2	3	1	4
(d)	3	4	1	2

Darken your choice with HB Pencil

1. ⓐ ⓑ ⓒ ⓓ	10. ⓐ ⓑ ⓒ ⓓ	19. ⓐ ⓑ ⓒ ⓓ	28. ⓐ ⓑ ⓒ ⓓ	37. ⓐ ⓑ ⓒ ⓓ	46. ⓐ ⓑ ⓒ ⓓ
2. ⓐ ⓑ ⓒ ⓓ	11. ⓐ ⓑ ⓒ ⓓ	20. ⓐ ⓑ ⓒ ⓓ	29. ⓐ ⓑ ⓒ ⓓ	38. ⓐ ⓑ ⓒ ⓓ	47. ⓐ ⓑ ⓒ ⓓ
3. ⓐ ⓑ ⓒ ⓓ	12. ⓐ ⓑ ⓒ ⓓ	21. ⓐ ⓑ ⓒ ⓓ	30. ⓐ ⓑ ⓒ ⓓ	39. ⓐ ⓑ ⓒ ⓓ	48. ⓐ ⓑ ⓒ ⓓ
4. ⓐ ⓑ ⓒ ⓓ	13. ⓐ ⓑ ⓒ ⓓ	22. ⓐ ⓑ ⓒ ⓓ	31. ⓐ ⓑ ⓒ ⓓ	40. ⓐ ⓑ ⓒ ⓓ	49. ⓐ ⓑ ⓒ ⓓ
5. ⓐ ⓑ ⓒ ⓓ	14. ⓐ ⓑ ⓒ ⓓ	23. ⓐ ⓑ ⓒ ⓓ	32. ⓐ ⓑ ⓒ ⓓ	41. ⓐ ⓑ ⓒ ⓓ	50. ⓐ ⓑ ⓒ ⓓ
6. ⓐ ⓑ ⓒ ⓓ	15. ⓐ ⓑ ⓒ ⓓ	24. ⓐ ⓑ ⓒ ⓓ	33. ⓐ ⓑ ⓒ ⓓ	42. ⓐ ⓑ ⓒ ⓓ	
7. ⓐ ⓑ ⓒ ⓓ	16. ⓐ ⓑ ⓒ ⓓ	25. ⓐ ⓑ ⓒ ⓓ	34. ⓐ ⓑ ⓒ ⓓ	43. ⓐ ⓑ ⓒ ⓓ	
8. ⓐ ⓑ ⓒ ⓓ	17. ⓐ ⓑ ⓒ ⓓ	26. ⓐ ⓑ ⓒ ⓓ	35. ⓐ ⓑ ⓒ ⓓ	44. ⓐ ⓑ ⓒ ⓓ	
9. ⓐ ⓑ ⓒ ⓓ	18. ⓐ ⓑ ⓒ ⓓ	27. ⓐ ⓑ ⓒ ⓓ	36. ⓐ ⓑ ⓒ ⓓ	45. ⓐ ⓑ ⓒ ⓓ	

Answer Sheet

Chapter 01

1. (a)	2. (b)	3. (c)	4. (d)	5. (b)	6. (a)	7. (b)	8. (a)	9. (c)	10. (d)
11. (a)	12. (b)	13. (c)	14. (c)	15. (c)	16. (a)	17. (c)	18. (a)	19. (a)	20. (c)
21. (d)	22. (c)	23. (a)	24. (b)	25. (d)	26. (a)	27. (b)	28. (c)	29. (d)	30. (a)
31. (b)	32. (c)	33. (d)	34. (c)	35. (a)	36. (b)	37. (a)	38. (c)	39. (d)	40. (b)
41. (d)									

Chapter 02

1. (b)	2. (c)	3. (d)	4. (b)	5. (a)	6. (a)	7. (c)	8. (a)	9. (d)	10. (a)
11. (a)	12. (a)	13. (d)	14. (c)	15. (b)	16. (c)	17. (a)	18. (c)	19. (c)	20. (a)
21. (a)	22. (c)	23. (c)	24. (d)	25. (a)					

Chapter 03

1. (a)	2. (b)	3. (c)	4. (c)	5. (d)	6. (b)	7. (a)	8. (b)	9. (c)	10. (c)
11. (a)	12. (a)	13. (d)	14. (d)	15. (c)	16. (a)	17. (a)	18. (c)	19. (b)	20. (a)
21. (a)	22. (d)	23. (c)	24. (c)	25. (b)	26. (b)	27. (b)	28. (a)	29. (c)	

Chapter 04

1. (b)	2. (a)	3. (c)	4. (b)	5. (d)	6. (c)	7. (c)	8. (c)	9. (a)	10. (b)
11. (a)	12. (b)	13. (d)	14. (d)	15. (d)	16. (a)	17. (a)	18. (b)	19. (b)	20. (a)
21. (c)	22. (d)	23. (c)	24. (a)	25. (c)	26. (c)	27. (b)	28. (d)		

Chapter 05

1. (b)	2. (c)	3. (c)	4. (c)	5. (a)	6. (b)	7. (a)	8. (b)	9. (a)	10. (b)
11. (a)	12. (b)	13. (b)	14. (a)	15. (b)	16. (a)	17. (d)	18. (a)	19. (b)	20. (c)
21. (d)	22. (b)	23. (d)	24. (c)	25. (b)	26. (c)	27. (a)	28. (c)	29. (c)	30. (a)

Chapter 06

1. (a)	2. (b)	3. (a)	4. (d)	5. (a)	6. (b)	7. (a)	8. (b)	9. (c)	10. (d)
11. (b)	12. (d)	13. (d)	14. (a)	15. (d)	16. (a)	17. (b)	18. (a)	19. (c)	20. (b)
21. (c)	22. (a)	23. (b)	24. (c)	25. (d)	26. (a)	27. (b)	28. (b)	29. (a)	30. (b)
31. (b)									

Chapter 07

1. (a)	2. (c)	3. (d)	4. (a)	5. (b)	6. (c)	7. (a)	8. (b)	9. (c)	10. (b)
11. (a)	12. (c)	13. (b)	14. (c)	15. (d)	16. (c)	17. (a)	18. (d)	19. (d)	20. (a)
21. (c)	22. (d)	23. (d)	24. (d)	25. (b)	26. (a)	27. (c)	28. (a)	29. (c)	30. (d)
31. (a)	32. (d)	33. (a)	34. (c)	35. (b)	36. (a)	37. (a)	38. (c)	39. (d)	

Chapter 08

1. (c)	**2.** (c)	**3.** (c)	**4.** (a)	**5.** (b)	**6.** (a)	**7.** (a)	**8.** (d)	**9.** (a)	**10.** (c)
11. (a)	**12.** (b)	**13.** (b)	**14.** (b)	**15.** (a)	**16.** (d)	**17.** (a)	**18.** (c)	**19.** (b)	**20.** (d)
21. (a)	**22.** (a)	**23.** (c)	**24.** (b)	**25.** (d)	**26.** (a)	**27.** (b)	**28.** (b)	**29.** (c)	**30.** (c)
31. (c)	**32.** (b)	**33.** (c)	**34.** (a)	**35.** (c)	**36.** (a)				

Chapter 09

1. (a)	**2.** (c)	**3.** (b)	**4.** (c)	**5.** (c)	**6.** (a)	**7.** (b)	**8.** (d)	**9.** (c)	**10.** (c)
11. (d)	**12.** (b)	**13.** (b)	**14.** (c)	**15.** (d)	**16.** (b)	**17.** (d)	**18.** (c)	**19.** (a)	**20.** (b)
21. (d)	**22.** (b)	**23.** (c)	**24.** (a)	**25.** (c)	**26.** (a)	**27.** (b)	**28.** (c)		

Chapter 10

1. (b)	**2.** (c)	**3.** (a)	**4.** (c)	**5.** (a)	**6.** (b)	**7.** (b)	**8.** (b)	**9.** (c)	**10.** (c)
11. (d)	**12.** (d)	**13.** (c)	**14.** (c)	**15.** (c)	**16.** (b)	**17.** (a)	**18.** (b)	**19.** (d)	**20.** (a)
21. (c)	**22.** (a)	**23.** (a)	**24.** (a)	**25.** (c)	**26.** (b)	**27.** (a)			

Chapter 11

1. (a)	**2.** (a)	**3.** (c)	**4.** (c)	**5.** (c)	**6.** (b)	**7.** (a)	**8.** (b)	**9.** (c)	**10.** (a)
11. (c)	**12.** (d)	**13.** (b)	**14.** (a)	**15.** (c)	**16.** (a)	**17.** (d)	**18.** (d)	**19.** (a)	**20.** (a)
21. (a)	**22.** (d)	**23.** (b)	**24.** (d)	**25.** (b)	**26.** (a)	**27.** (c)	**28.** (b)	**29.** (b)	**30.** (d)

Chapter 12

1. (d)	**2.** (b)	**3.** (b)	**4.** (b)	**5.** (c)	**6.** (b)	**7.** (b)	**8.** (b)	**9.** (a)	**10.** (d)
11. (c)	**12.** (c)	**13.** (c)	**14.** (b)	**15.** (d)	**16.** (b)	**17.** (b)	**18.** (c)	**19.** (b)	**20.** (c)
21. (b)	**22.** (b)	**23.** (b)	**24.** (c)	**25.** (a)	**26.** (a)	**27.** (b)			

Chapter 13

1. (a)	**2.** (a)	**3.** (a)	**4.** (a)	**5.** (b)	**6.** (a)	**7.** (c)	**8.** (c)	**9.** (a)	**10.** (b)
11. (d)	**12.** (b)	**13.** (b)	**14.** (c)	**15.** (d)	**16.** (d)	**17.** (c)	**18.** (a)	**19.** (a)	**20.** (c)
21. (a)	**22.** (b)	**23.** (c)	**24.** (c)						

Chapter 14

1. (c)	**2.** (a)	**3.** (d)	**4.** (d)	**5.** (d)	**6.** (a)	**7.** (b)	**8.** (a)	**9.** (b)	**10.** (c)
11. (b)	**12.** (a)	**13.** (d)	**14.** (d)	**15.** (a)	**16.** (a)	**17.** (b)	**18.** (d)	**19.** (b)	**20.** (b)
21. (d)	**22.** (a)	**23.** (b)	**24.** (b)	**25.** (d)	**26.** (a)	**27.** (b)	**28.** (c)	**29.** (d)	

Chapter 15

1. (c)	2. (c)	3. (b)	4. (b)	5. (c)	6. (b)	7. (a)	8. (c)	9. (c)	10. (d)
11. (c)	12. (a)	13. (a)	14. (a)	15. (b)	16. (c)	17. (b)	18. (a)	19. (a)	20. (c)
21. (b)	22. (b)	23. (c)	24. (b)	25. (a)	26. (a)	27. (b)	28. (b)	29. (c)	30. (a)
31. (d)	32. (a)	33. (b)	34. (b)	35. (a)					

Chapter 16

1. (a)	2. (c)	3. (a)	4. (b)	5. (b)	6. (a)	7. (b)	8. (a)	9. (c)	10. (c)
11. (c)	12. (a)	13. (a)	14. (c)	15. (c)	16. (c)	17. (b)	18. (d)	19. (c)	20. (d)
21. (d)	22. (d)	23. (d)	24. (c)	25. (b)					

Chapter 17

1. (a)	2. (c)	3. (a)	4. (c)	5. (b)	6. (a)	7. (d)	8. (b)	9. (c)	10. (a)
11. (d)	12. (a)	13. (c)	14. (a)	15. (a)	16. (a)	17. (d)	18. (a)	19. (a)	20. (b)
21. (b)	22. (b)	23. (c)	24. (a)	25. (c)	26. (c)	27. (c)	28. (c)	29. (c)	

Chapter 18

1. (d)	2. (b)	3. (a)	4. (d)	5. (b)	6. (a)	7. (c)	8. (d)	9. (a)	10. (a)
11. (c)	12. (c)	13. (b)	14. (b)	15. (b)	16. (d)	17. (c)	18. (b)	19. (a)	20. (b)
21. (b)	22. (a)	23. (c)	24. (c)						

Chapter 19

1. (b)	2. (b)	3. (c)	4. (a)	5. (b)	6. (a)	7. (b)	8. (d)	9. (a)	10. (c)
11. (a)	12. (a)	13. (a)	14. (a)	15. (b)	16. (b)	17. (b)	18. (d)	19. (c)	20. (b)
21. (a)	22. (a)	23. (a)	24. (b)	25. (c)	26. (c)	27. (a)	28. (b)	29. (b)	

Practice Set 01

1. (c)	2. (a)	3. (b)	4. (b)	5. (c)	6. (d)	7. (a)	8. (b)	9. (c)	10. (d)
11. (d)	12. (a)	13. (d)	14. (c)	15. (a)	16. (c)	17. (c)	18. (d)	19. (b)	20. (a)
21. (d)	22. (b)	23. (b)	24. (b)	25. (a)	26. (c)	27. (b)	28. (d)	29. (c)	30. (c)
31. (b)	32. (b)	33. (c)	34. (b)	35. (b)	36. (d)	37. (b)	38. (a)	39. (b)	40. (c)
41. (b)	42. (b)	43. (a)	44. (b)	45. (c)	46. (a)	47. (d)	48. (d)	49. (d)	50. (a)

Practice Set 02

1. (d)	2. (b)	3. (c)	4. (b)	5. (c)	6. (b)	7. (c)	8. (c)	9. (c)	10. (b)
11. (b)	12. (c)	13. (b)	14. (b)	15. (c)	16. (a)	17. (a)	18. (c)	19. (d)	20. (d)
21. (b)	22. (d)	23. (a)	24. (a)	25. (b)	26. (a)	27. (c)	28. (d)	29. (b)	30. (c)
31. (a)	32. (b)	33. (b)	34. (d)	35. (d)	36. (c)	37. (c)	38. (a)	39. (c)	40. (b)
41. (b)	42. (d)	43. (a)	44. (a)	45. (b)	46. (a)	47. (a)	48. (a)	49. (a)	50. (c)